Calmdalas
Adult Coloring Book #3

Over 50 Relaxing Mandalas to Color
One image per page

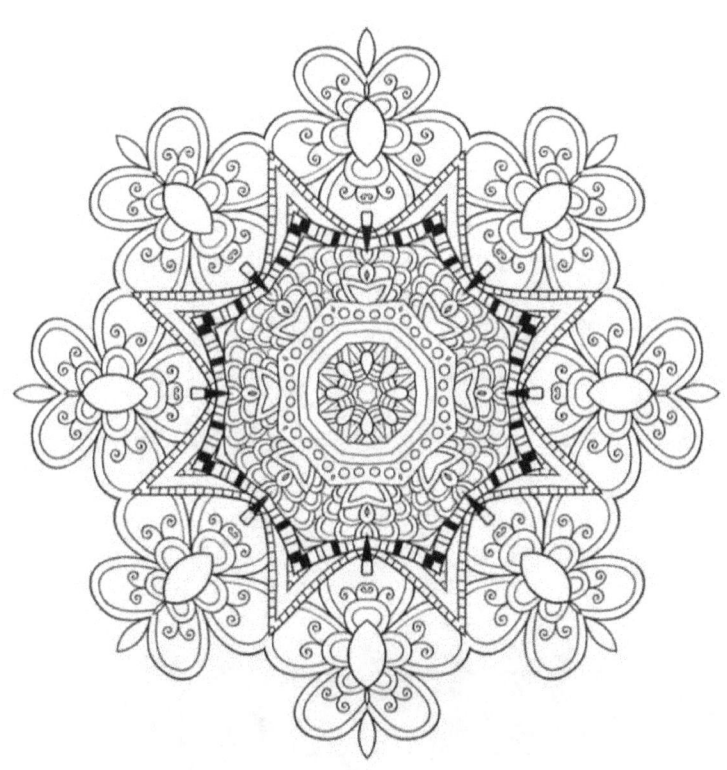

Go to www.calmdalas.com

Get notified about new books and get 10 **FREE** Calmdalas!

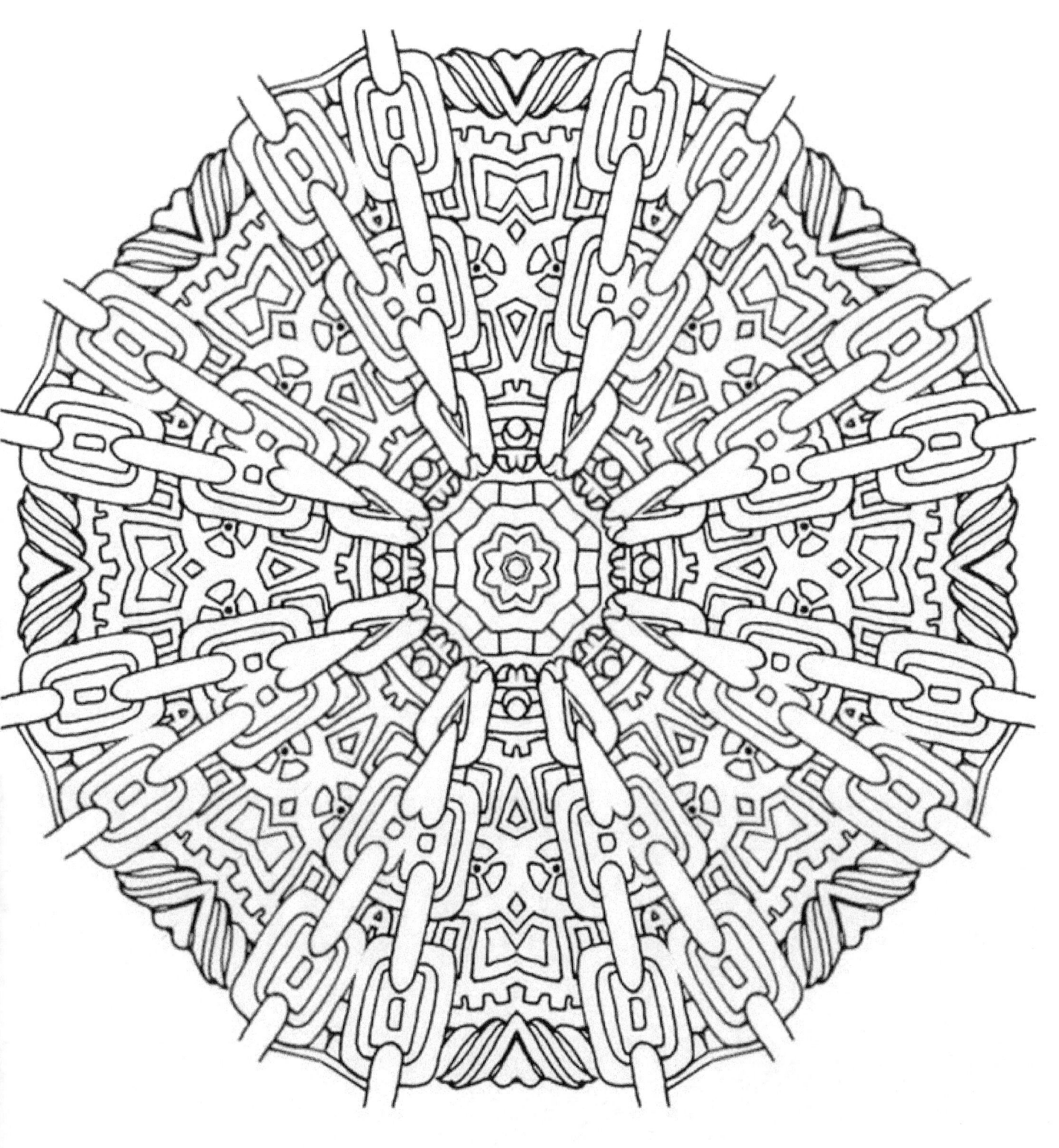

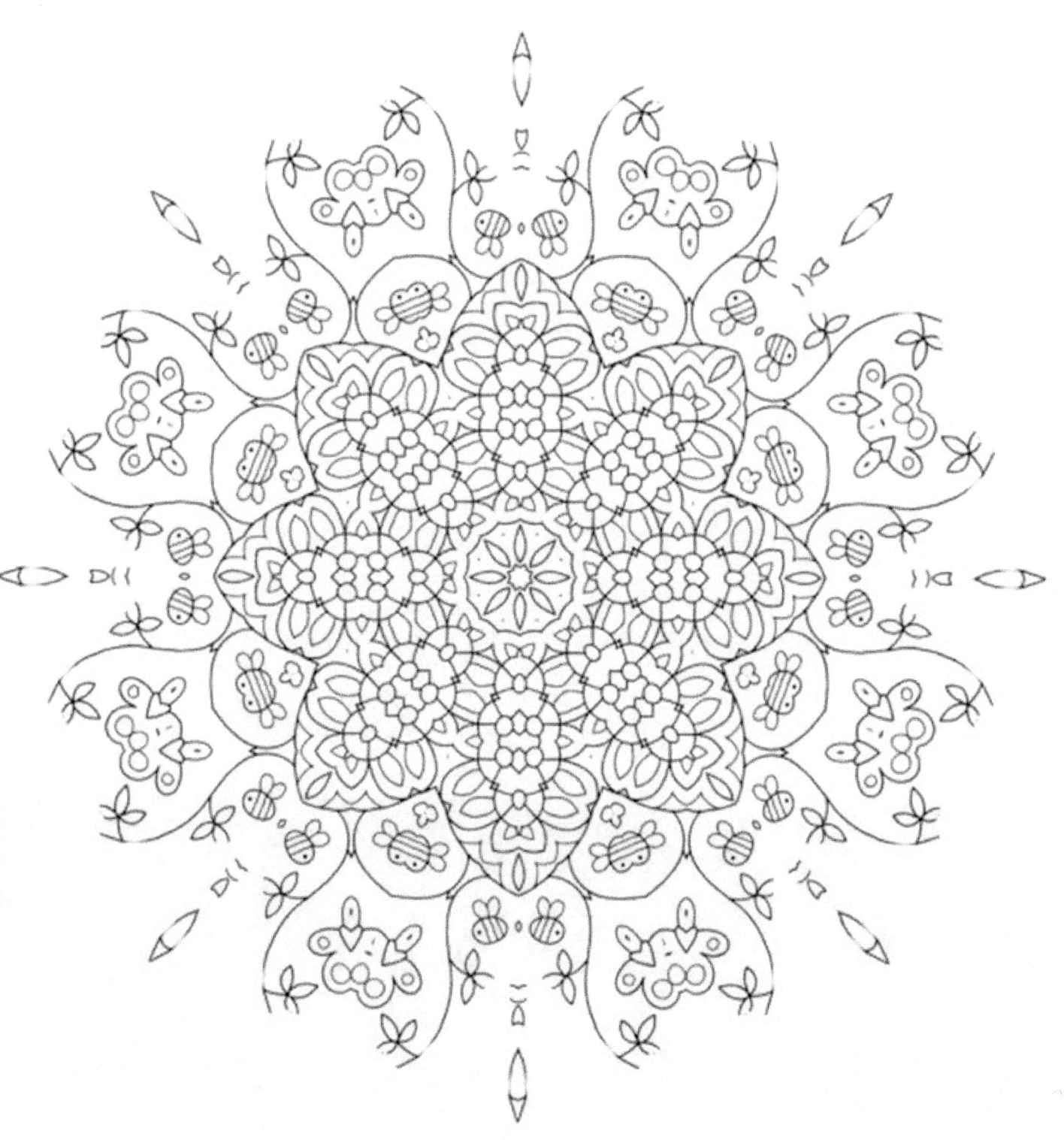

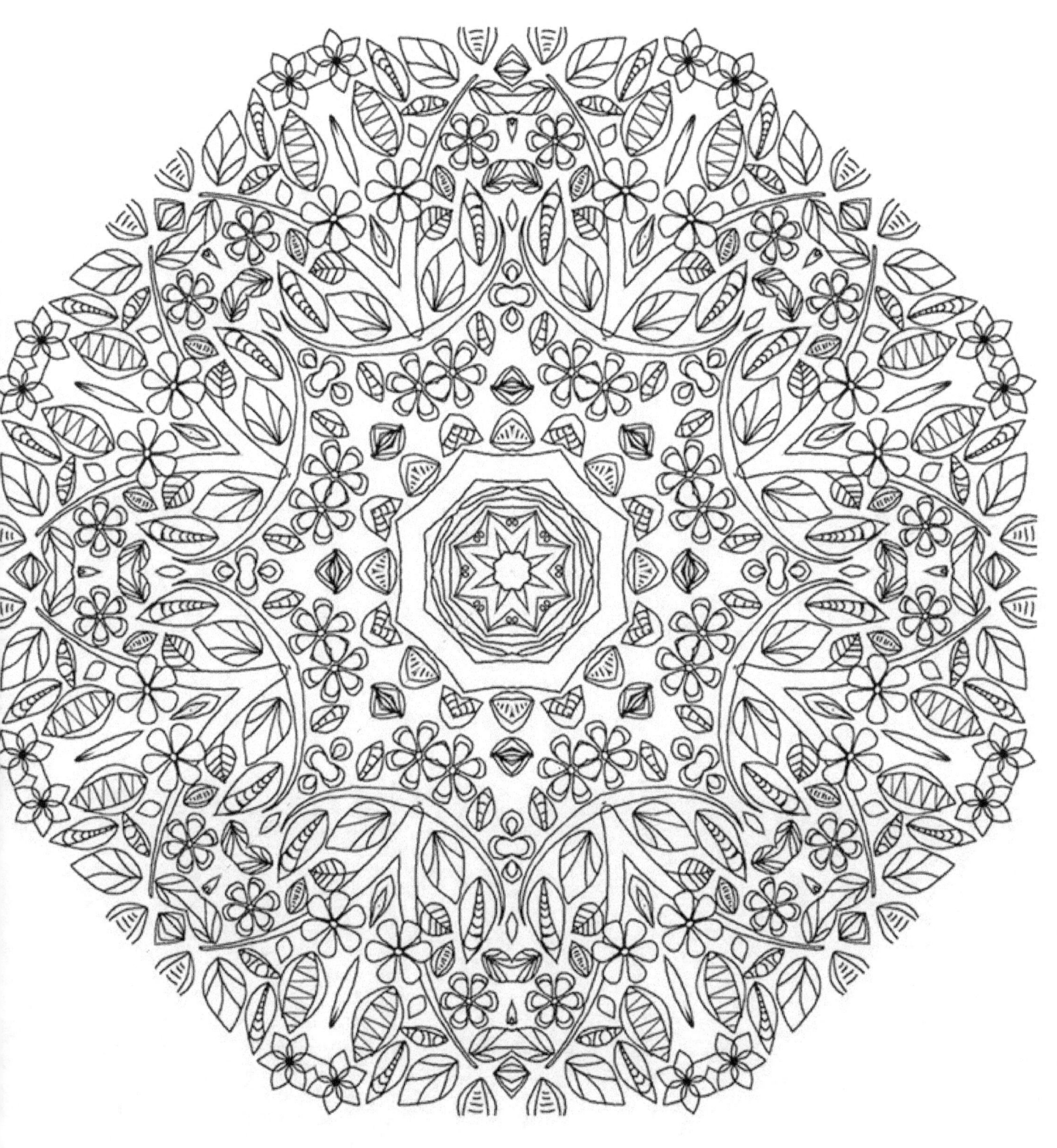

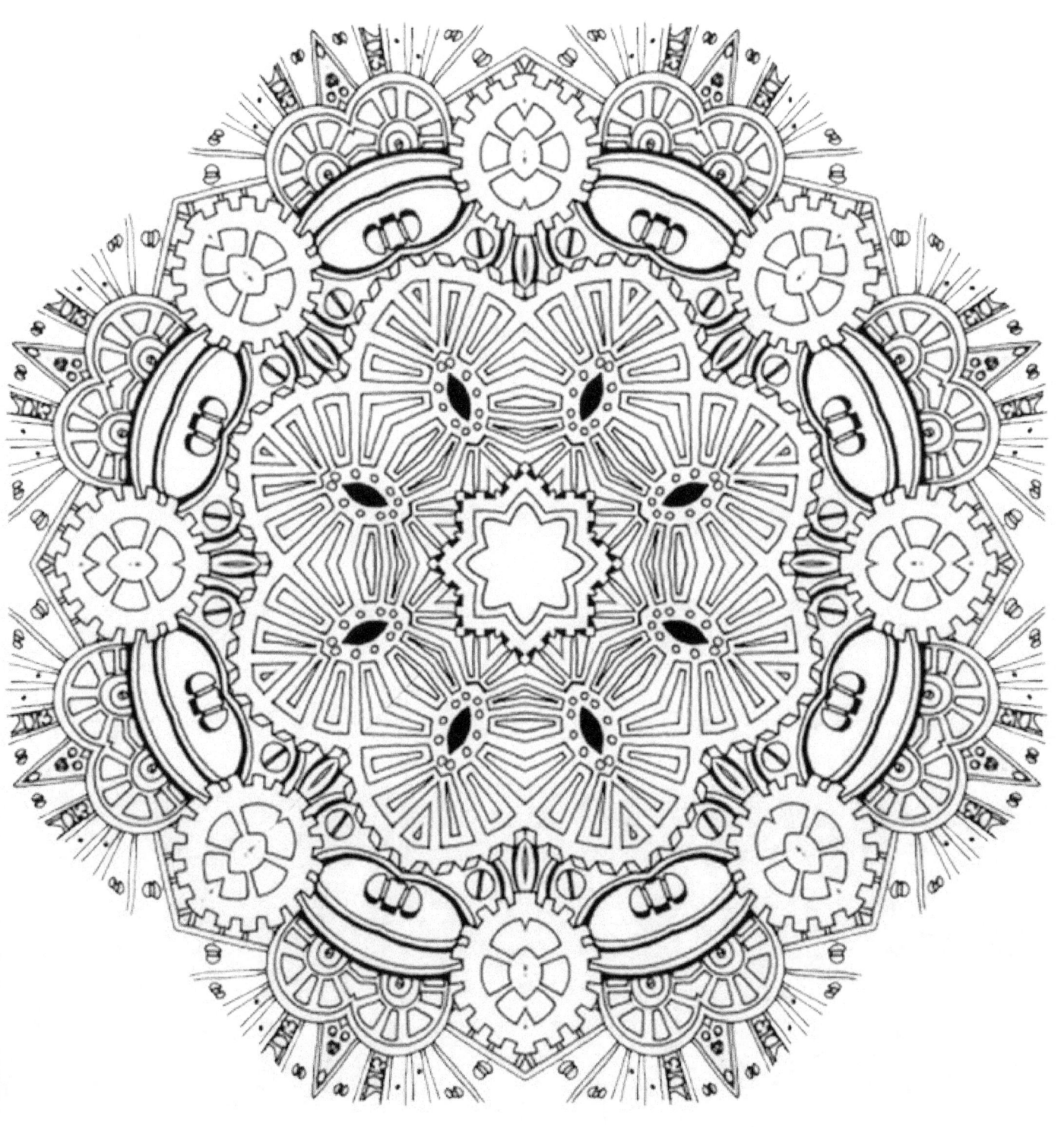

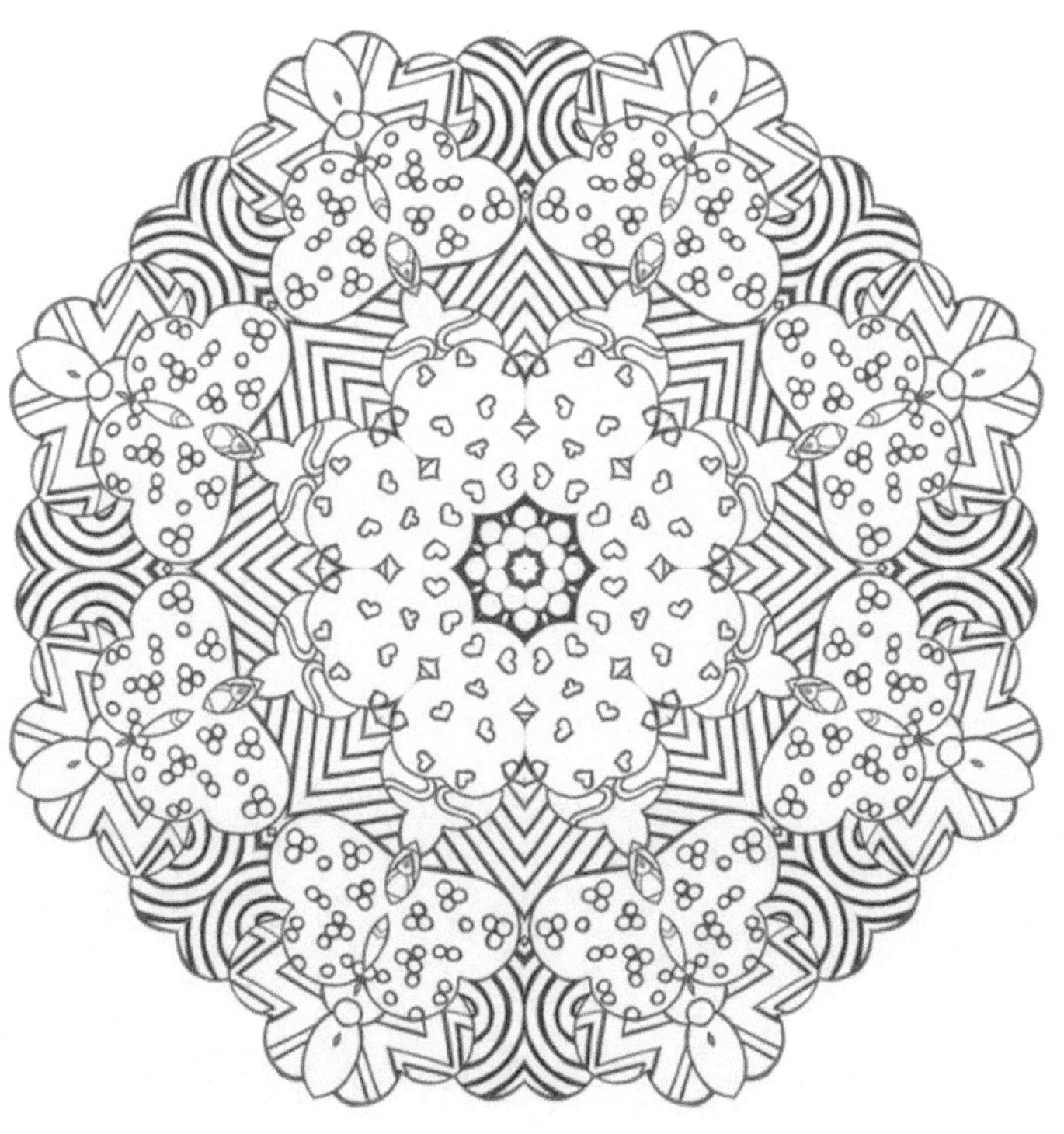

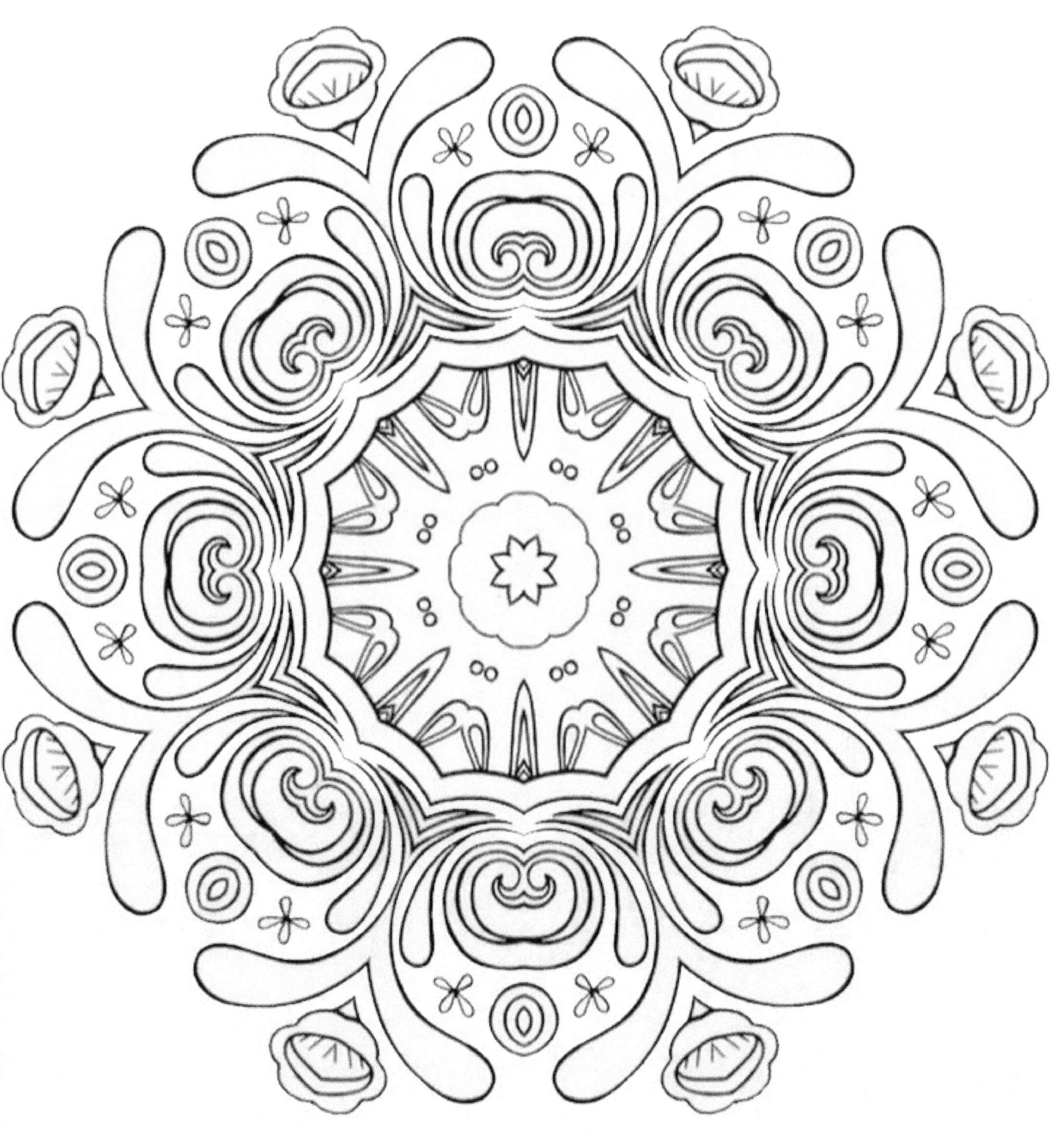

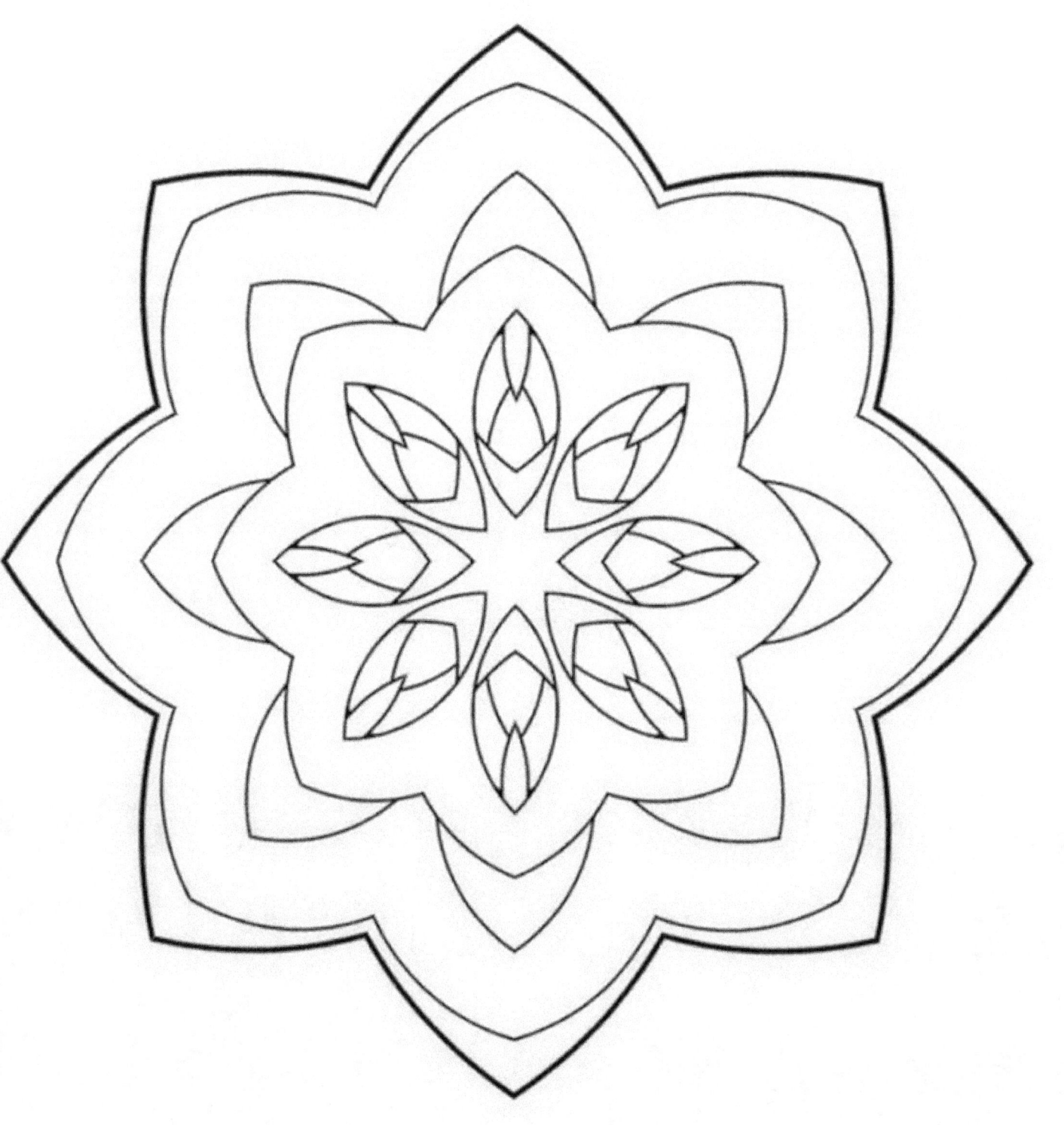

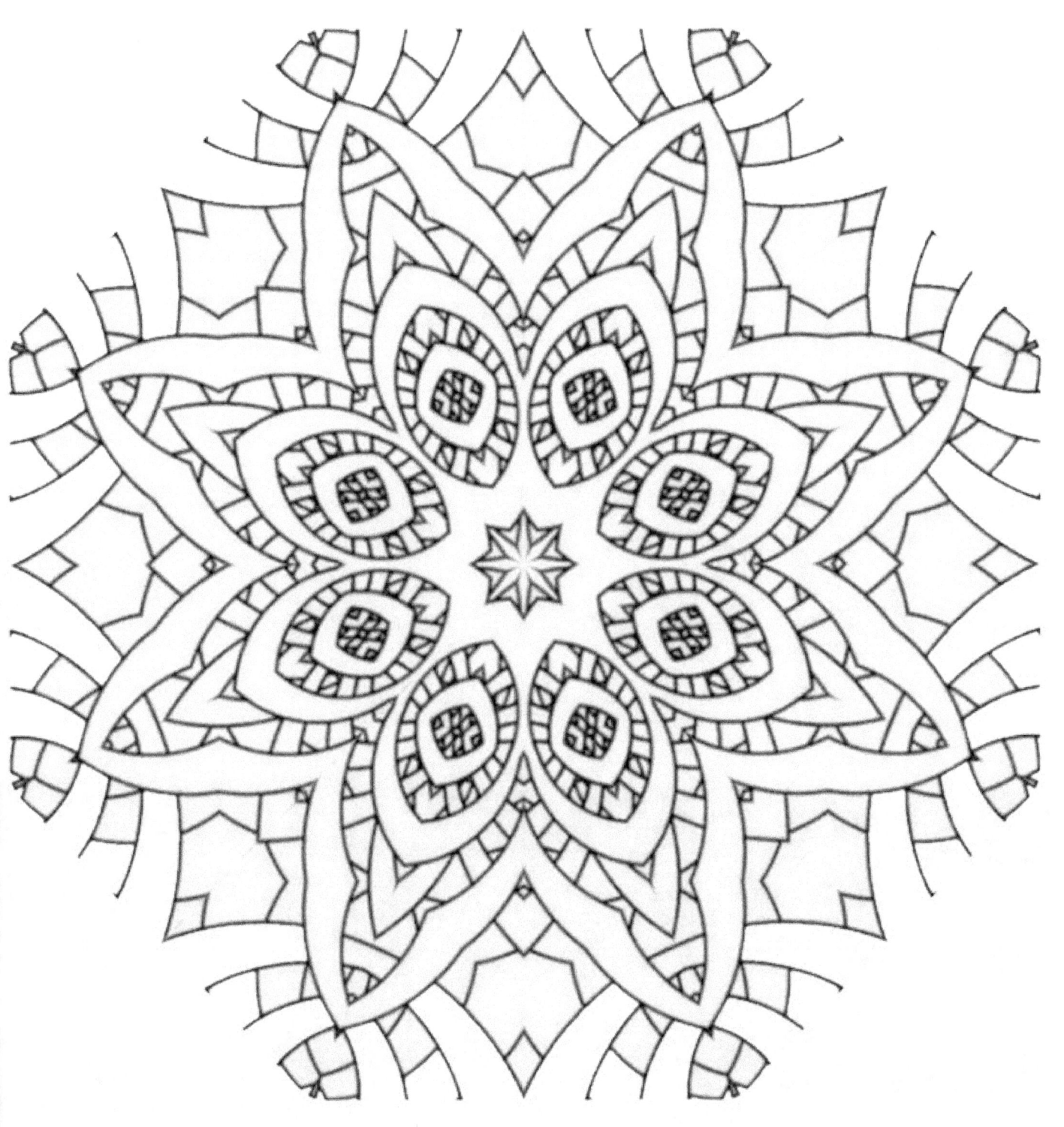

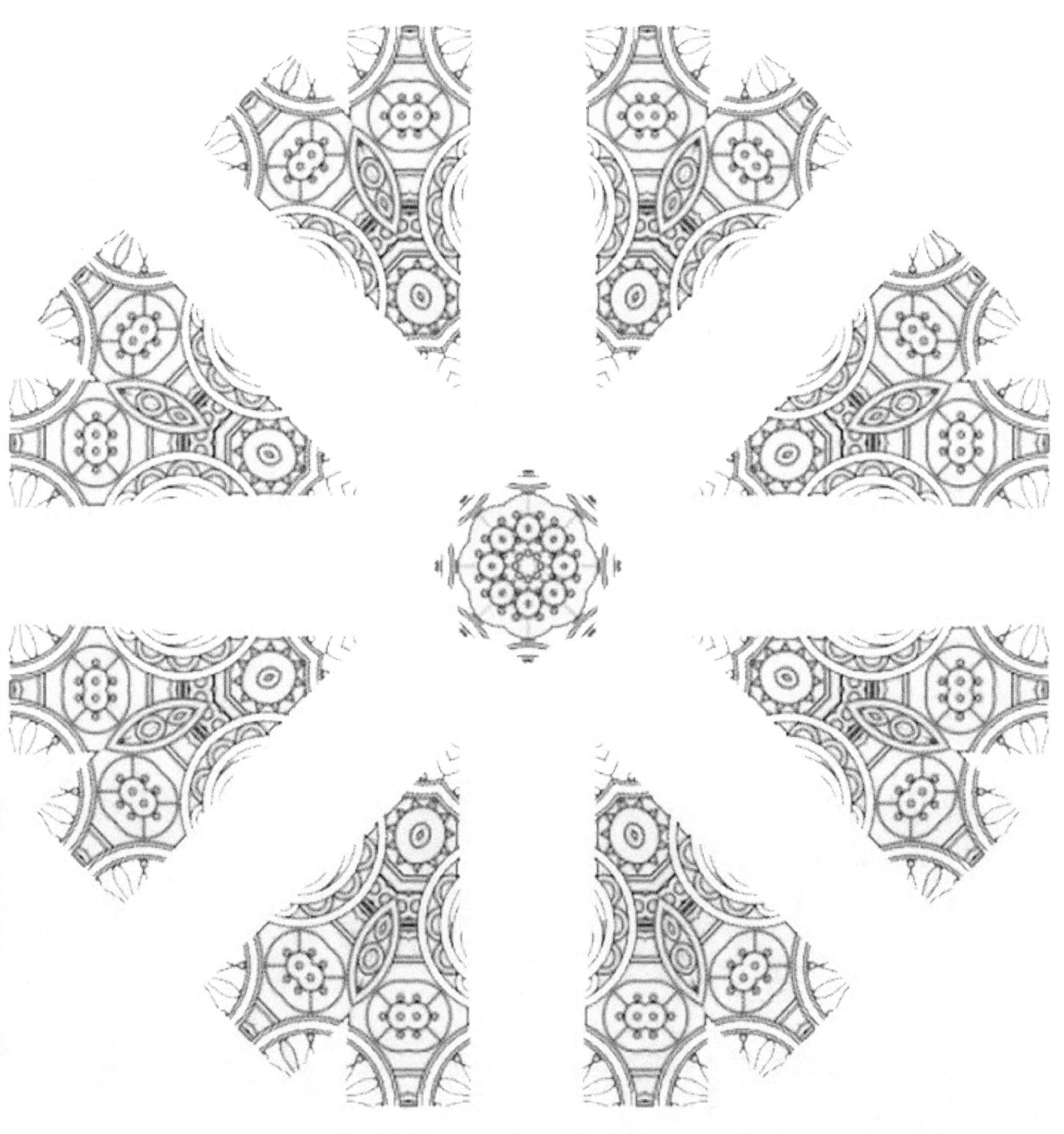

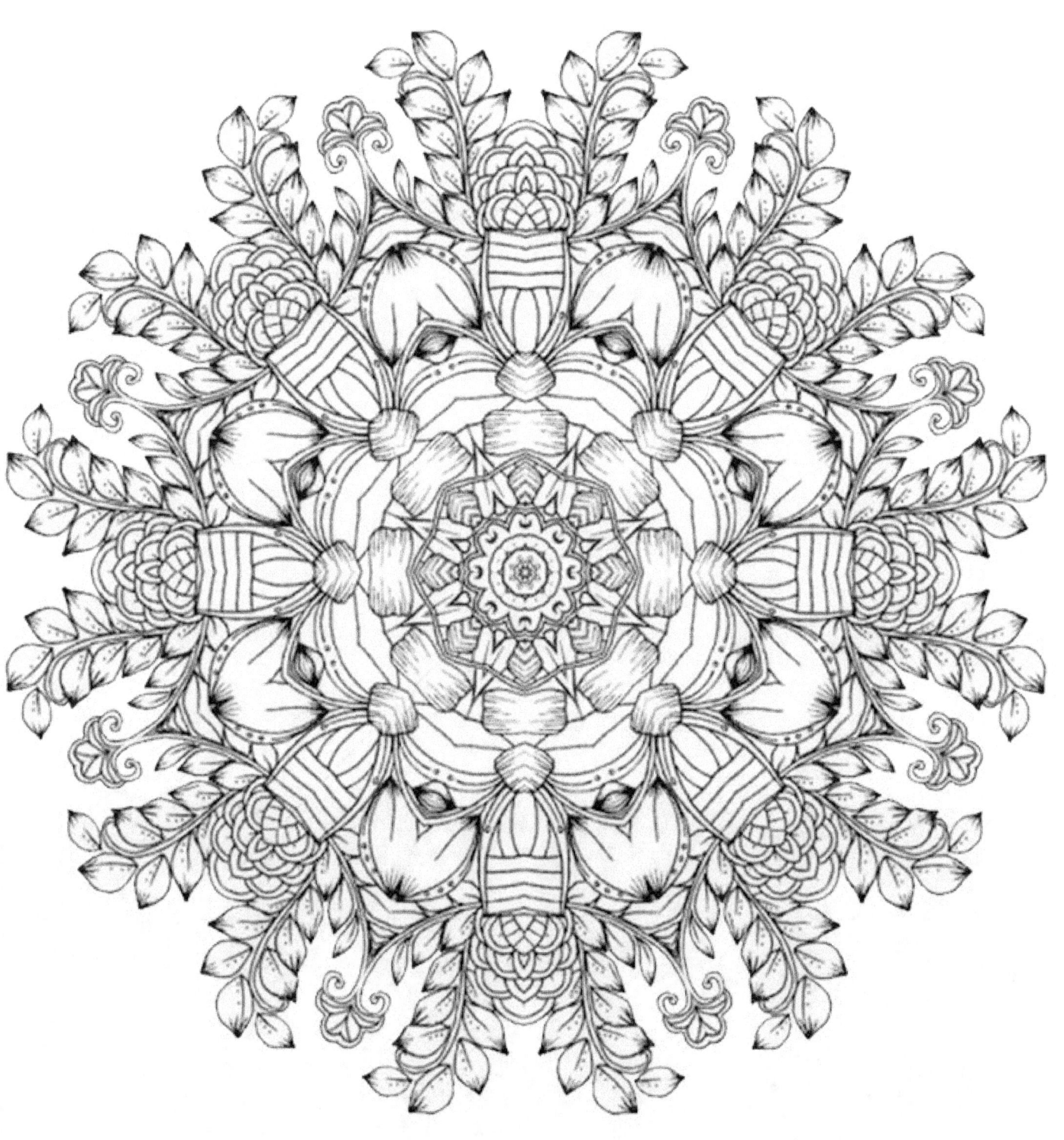

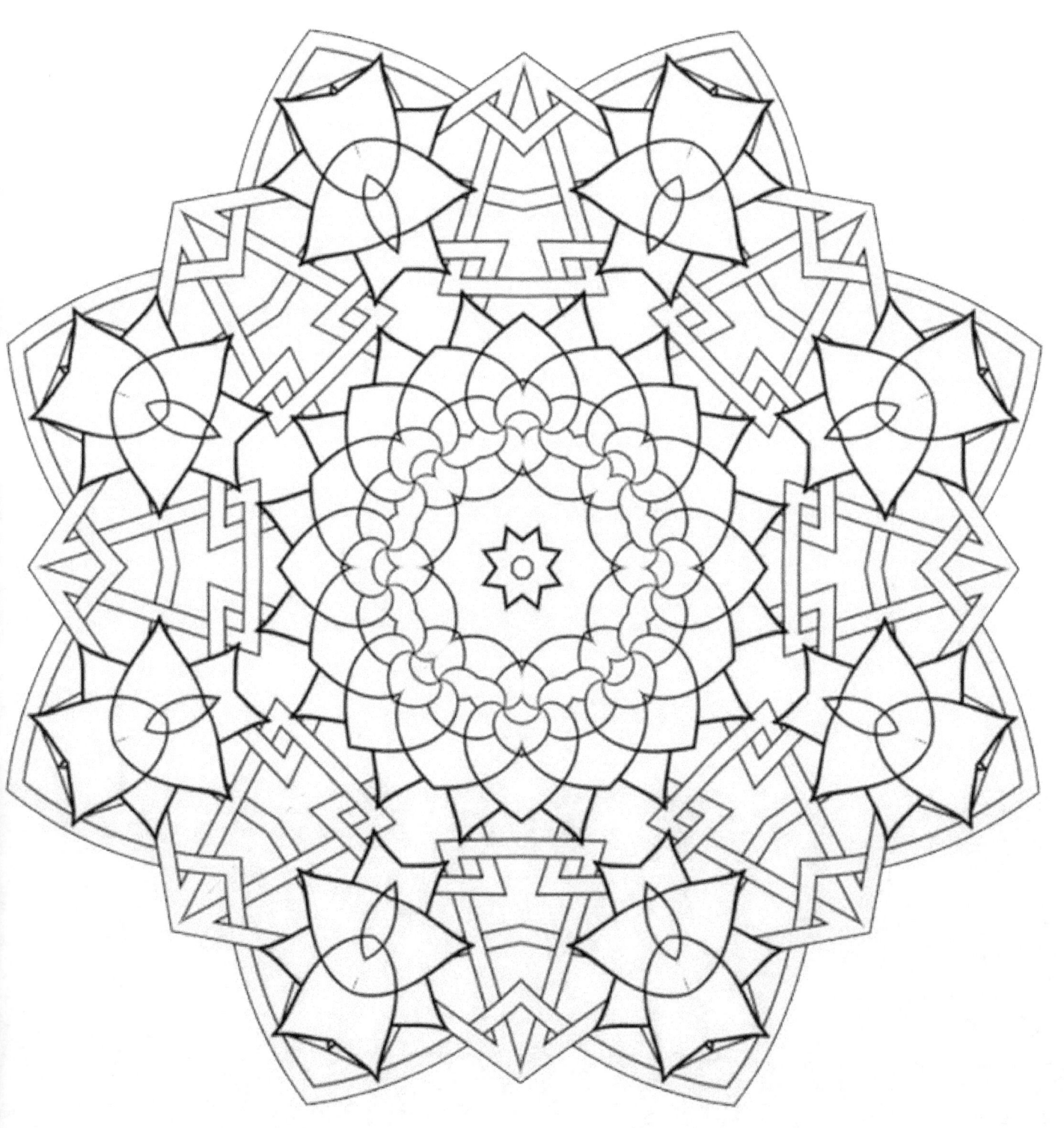

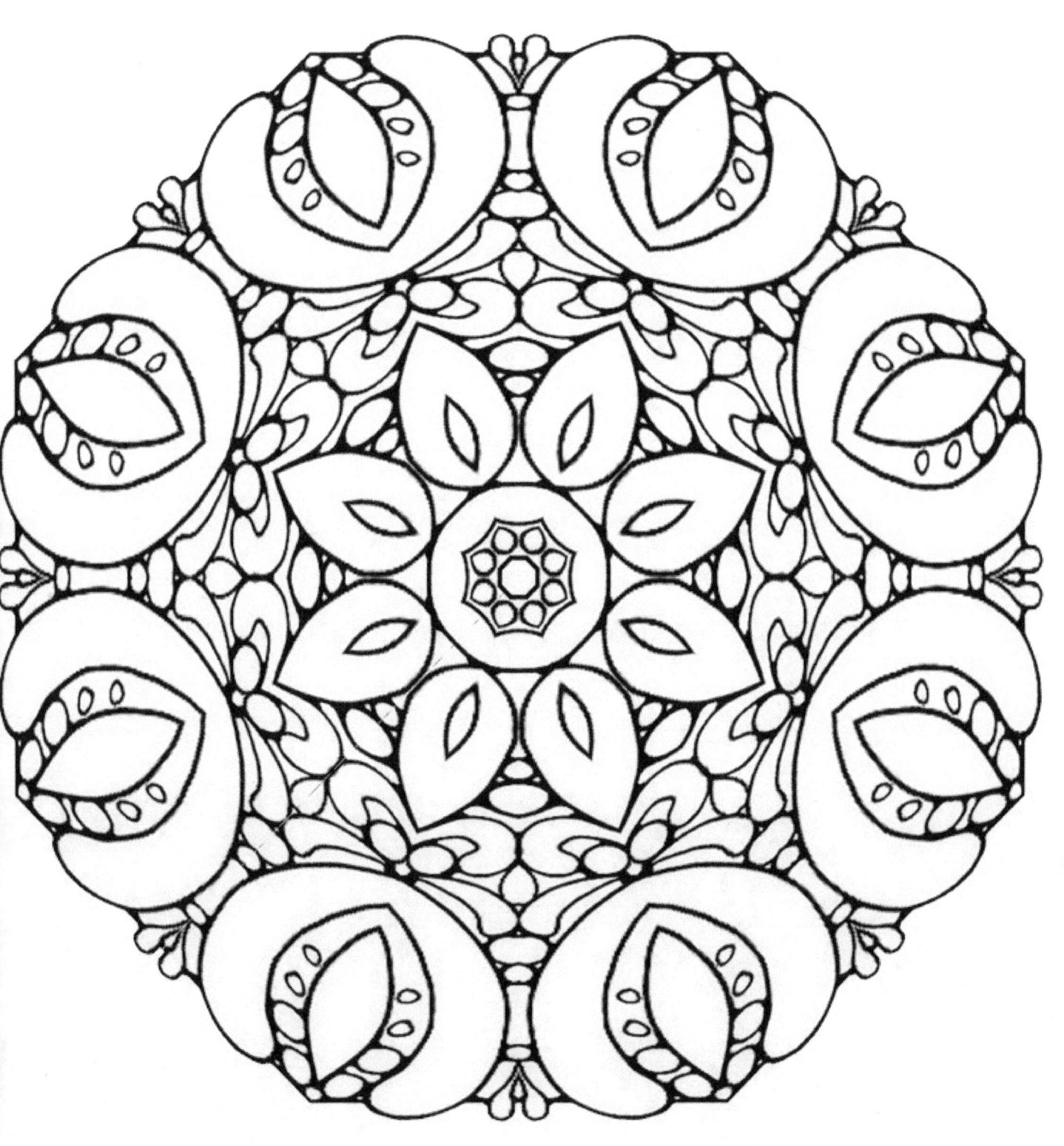

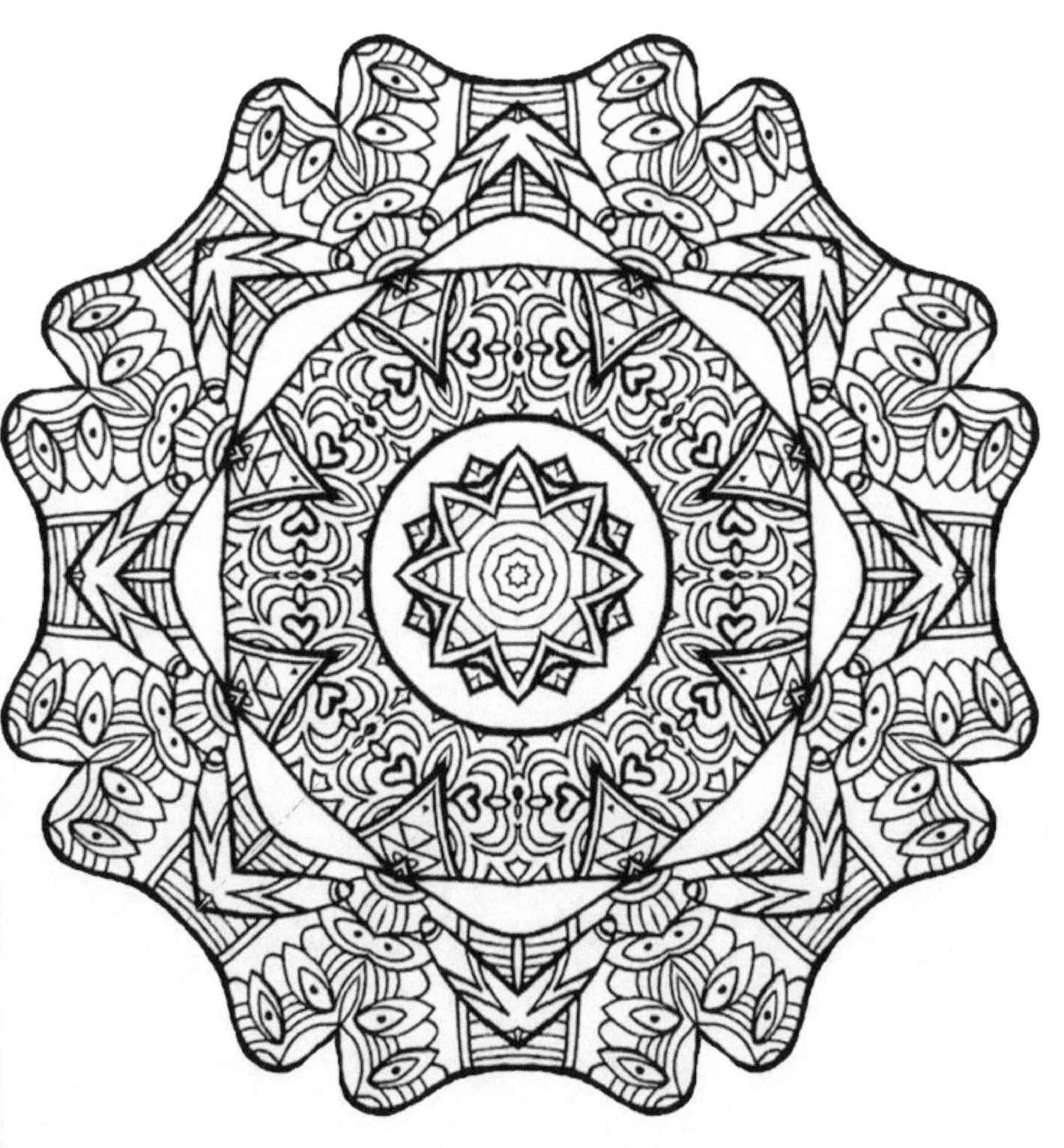

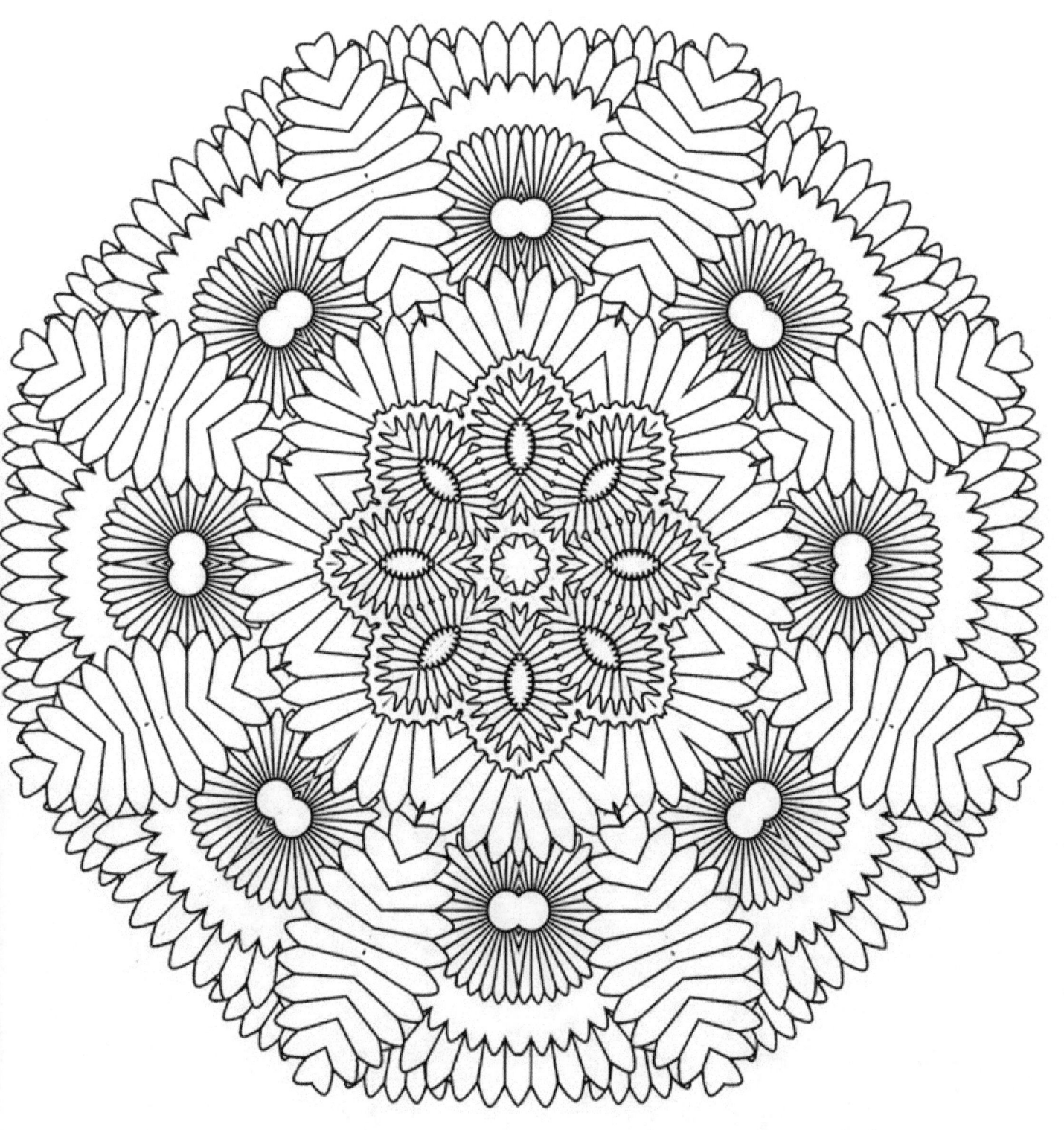

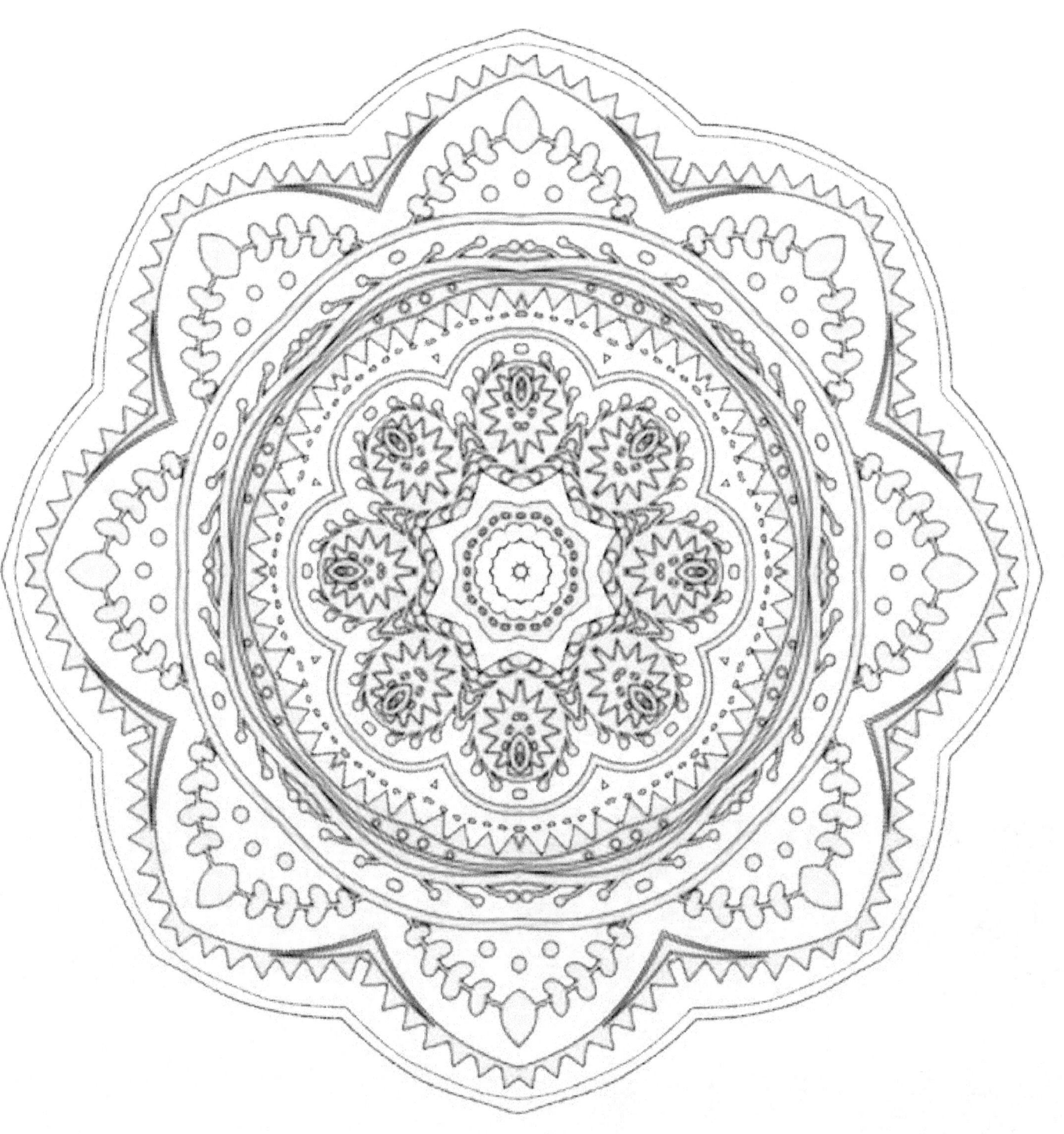

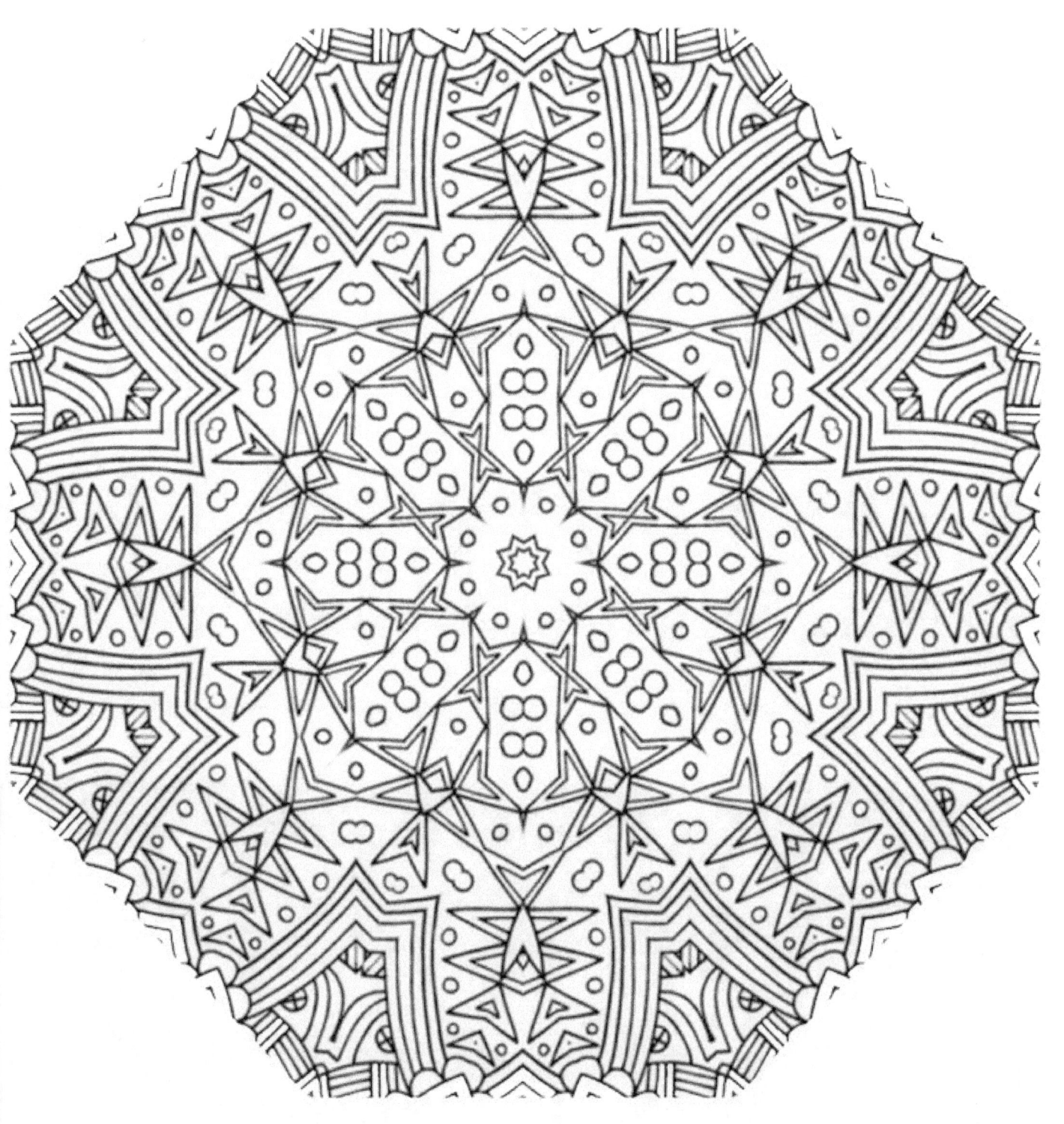

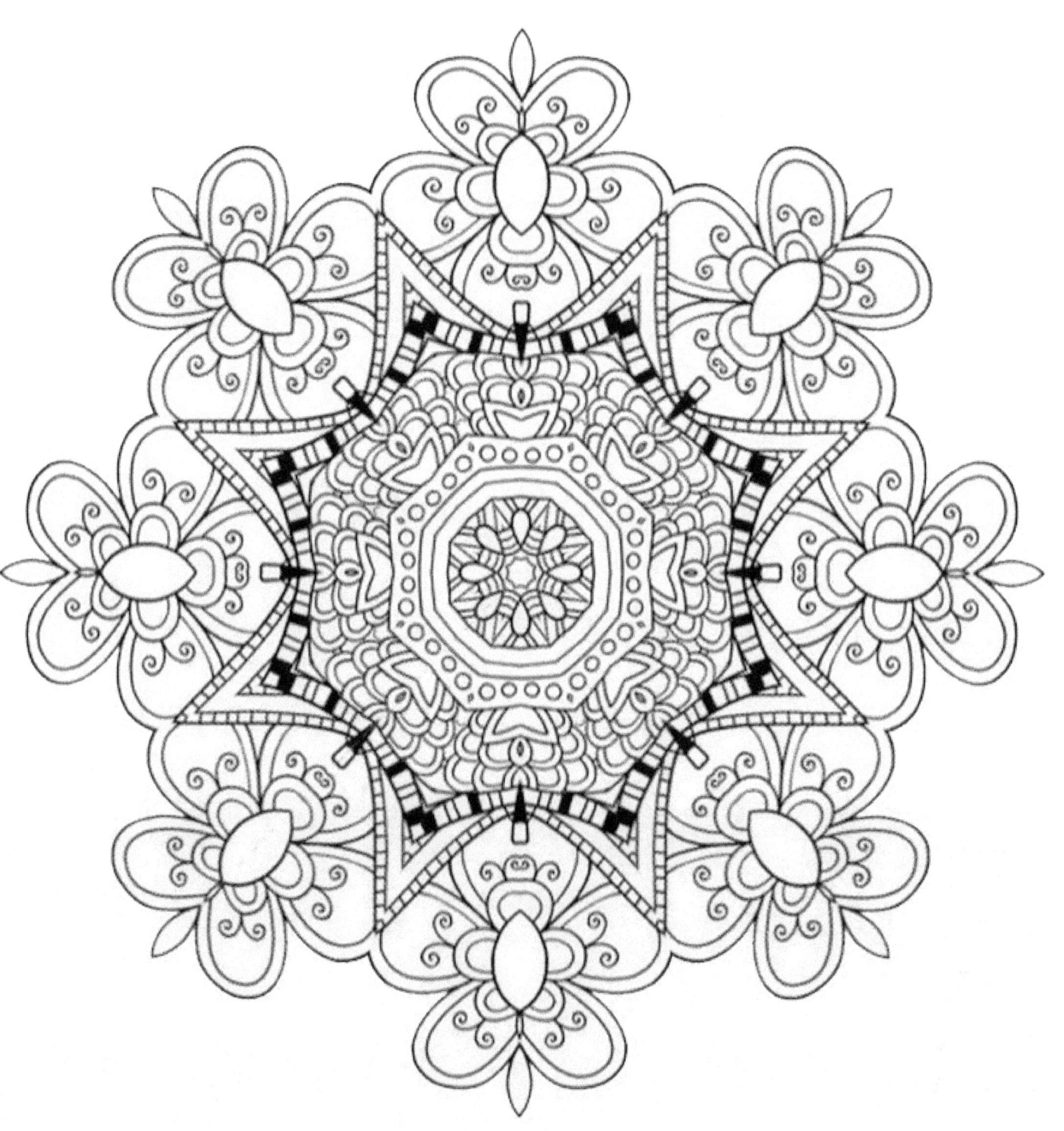

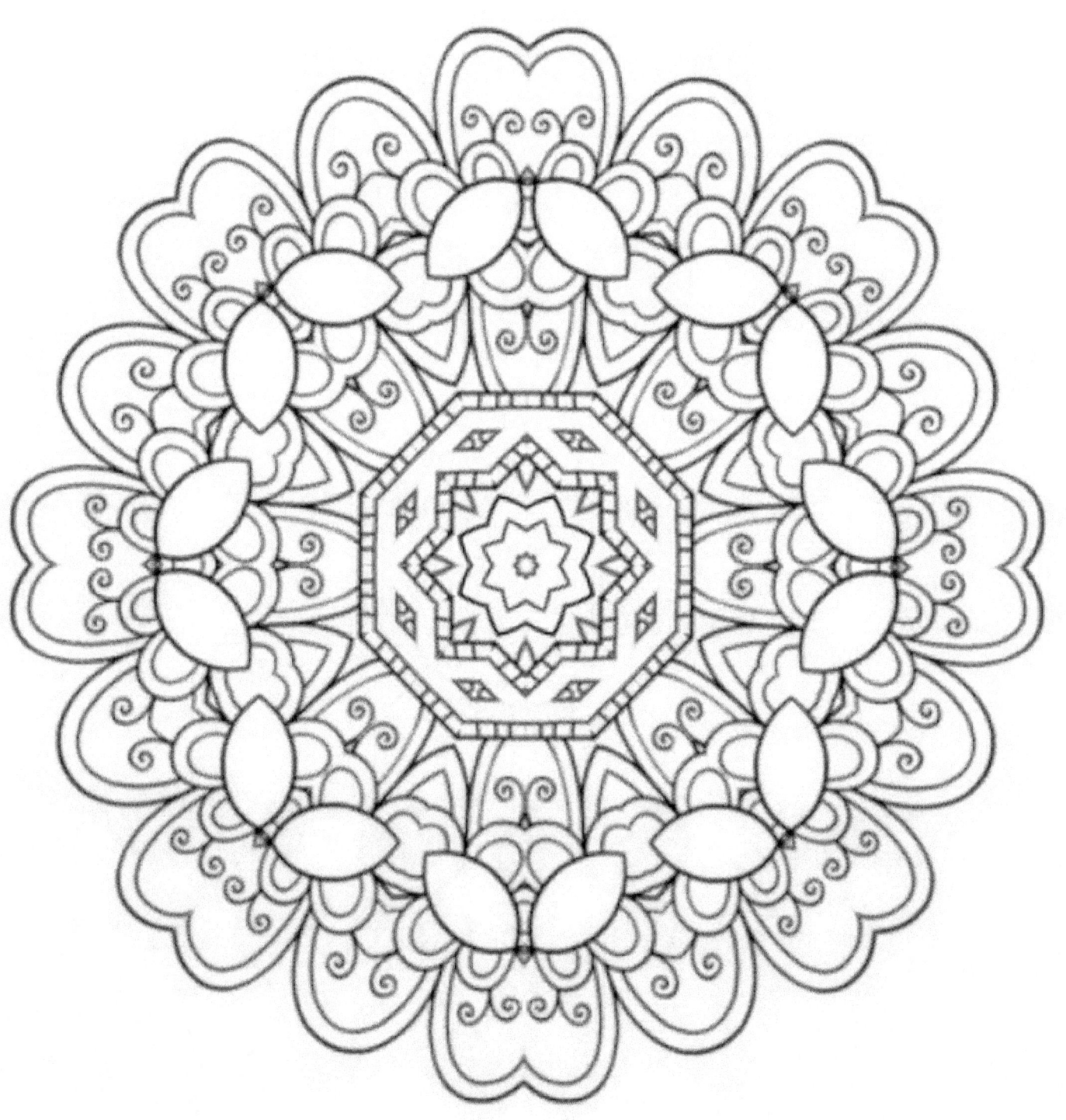

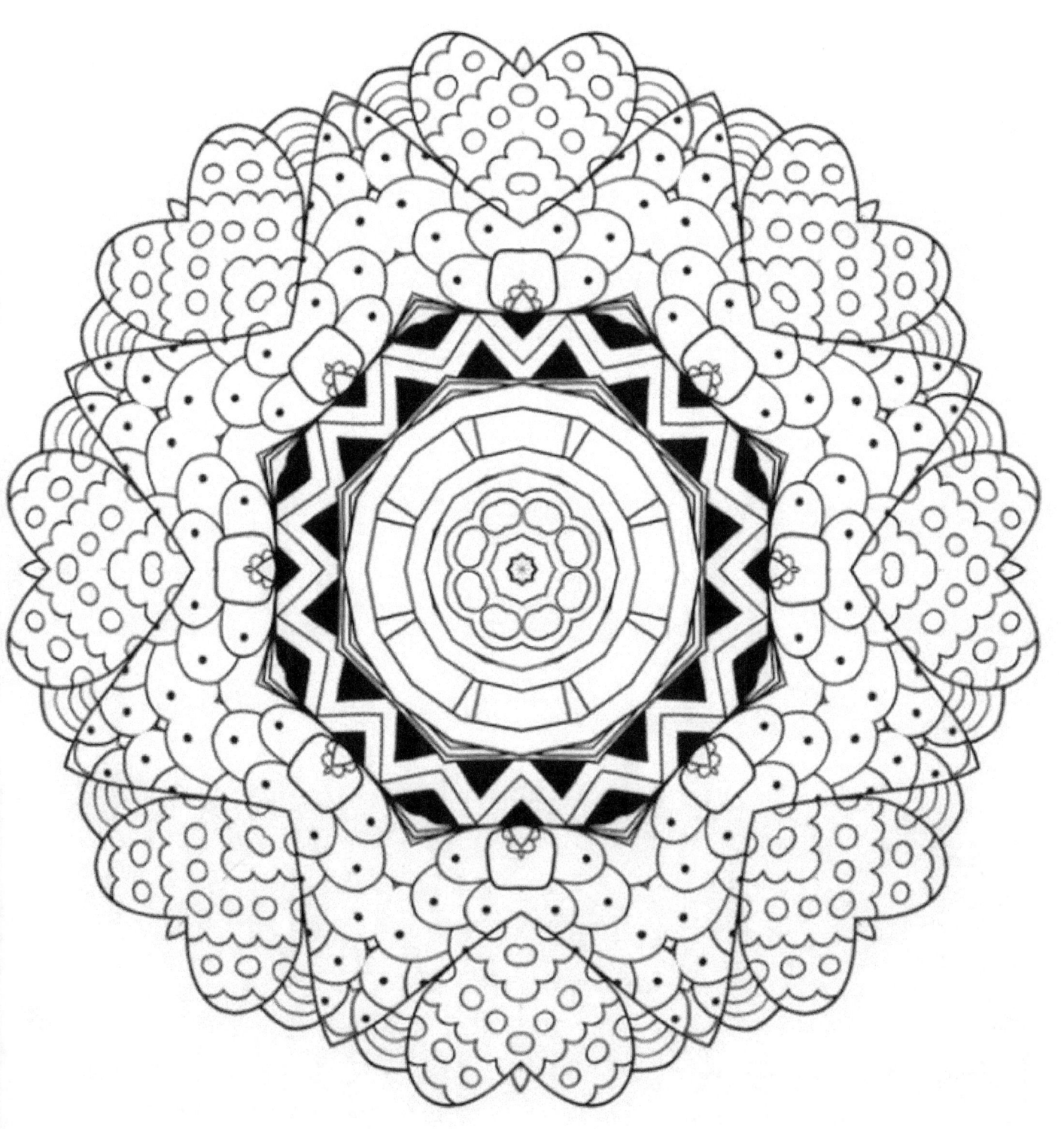

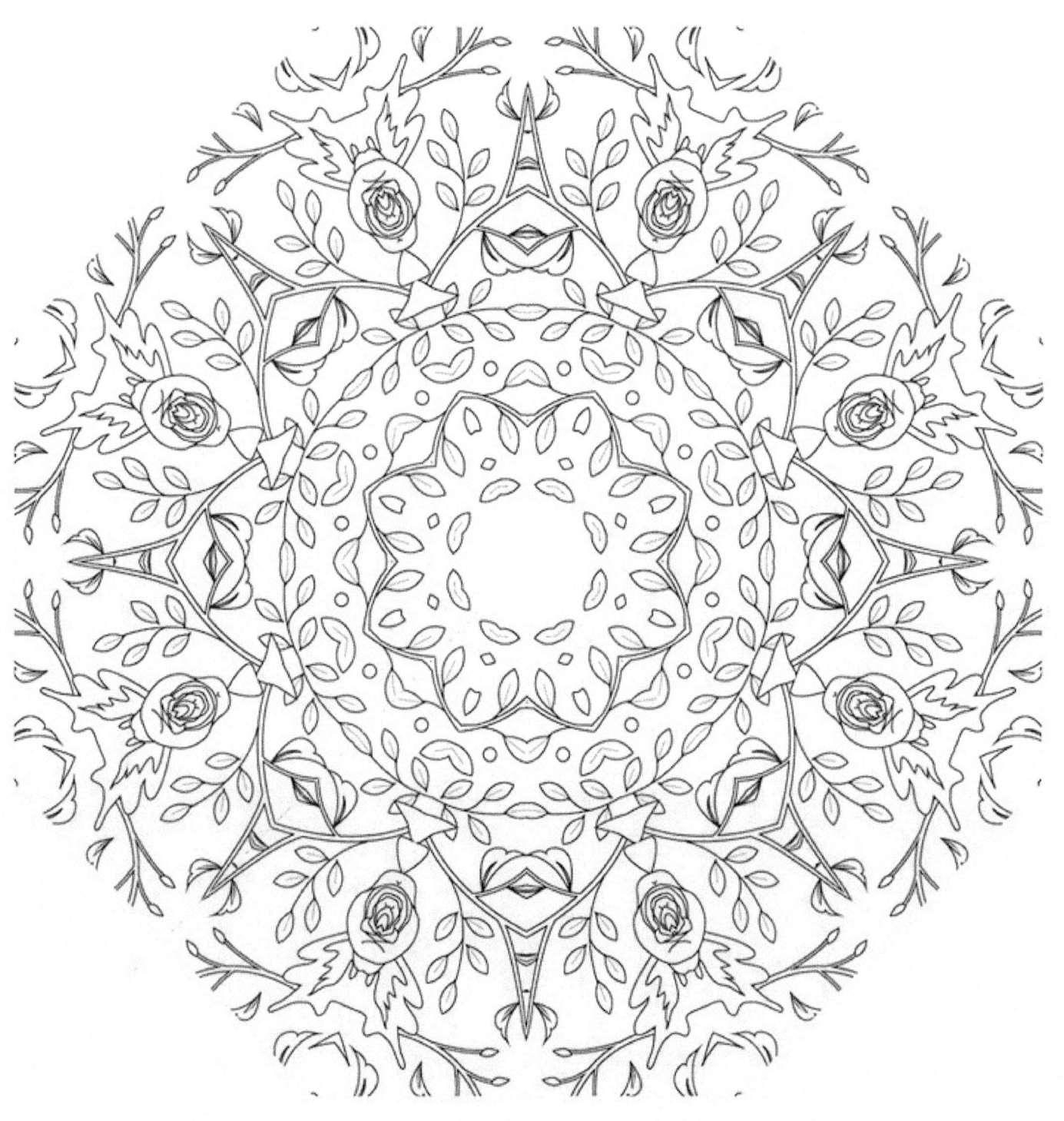

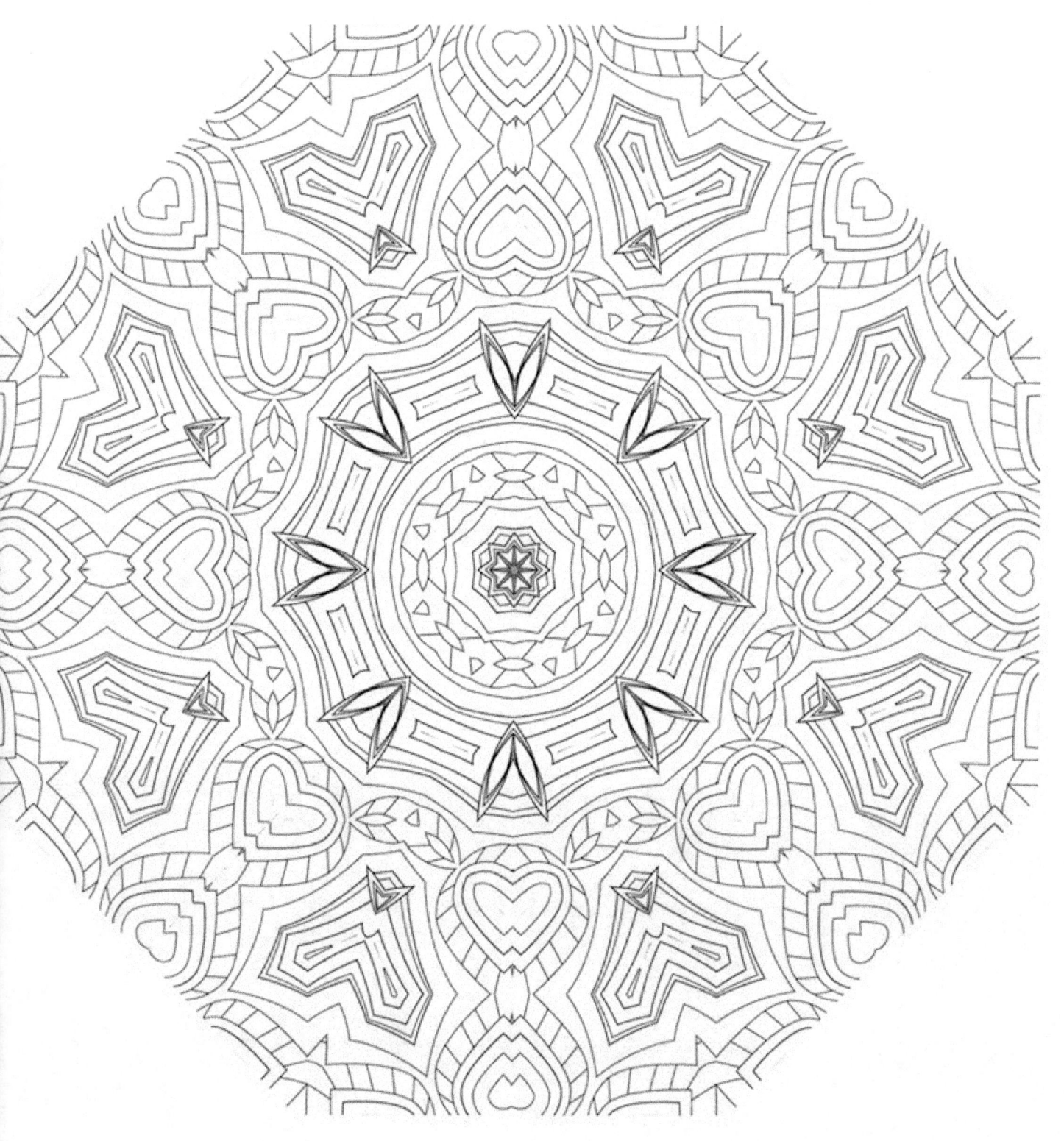

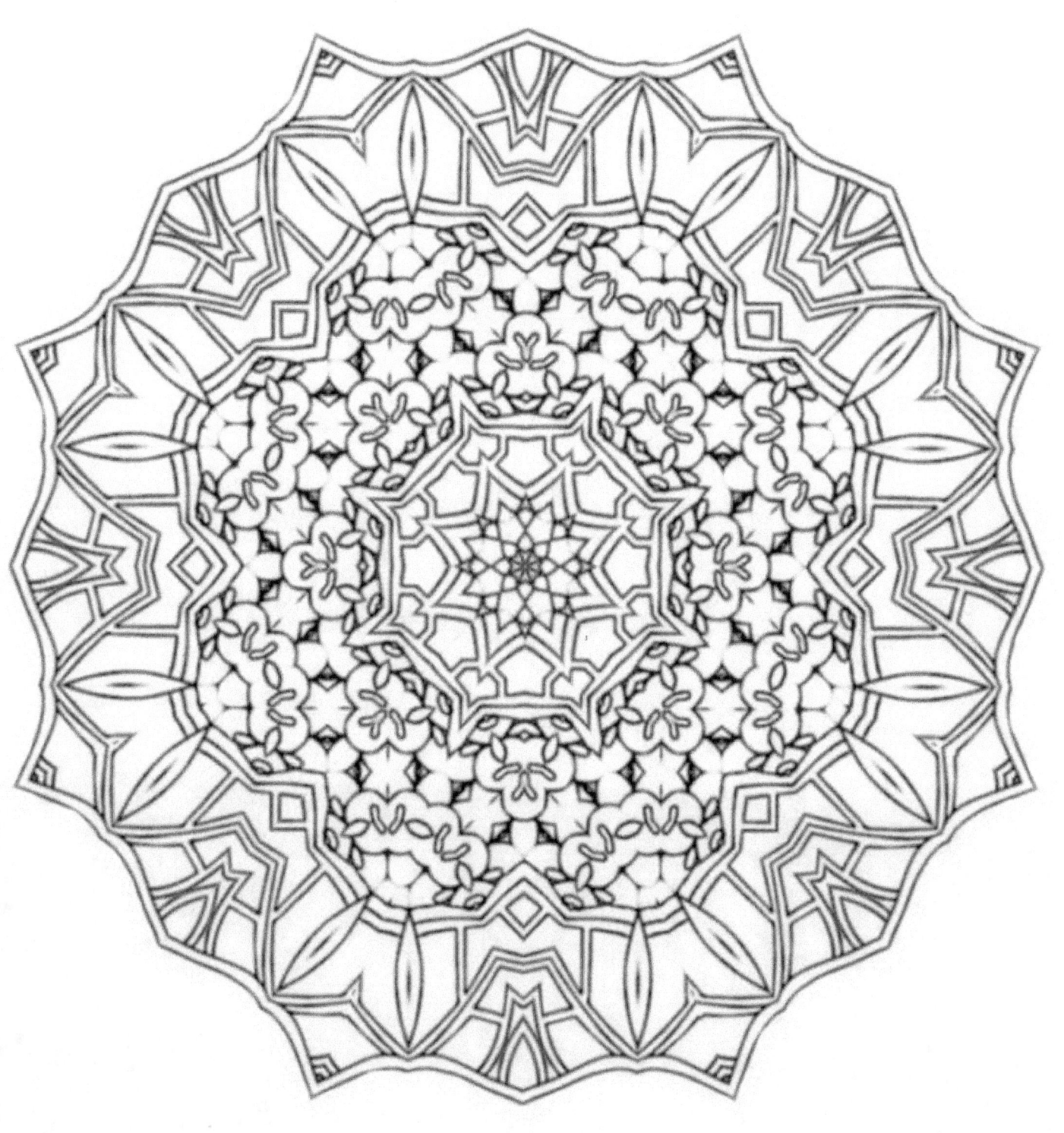

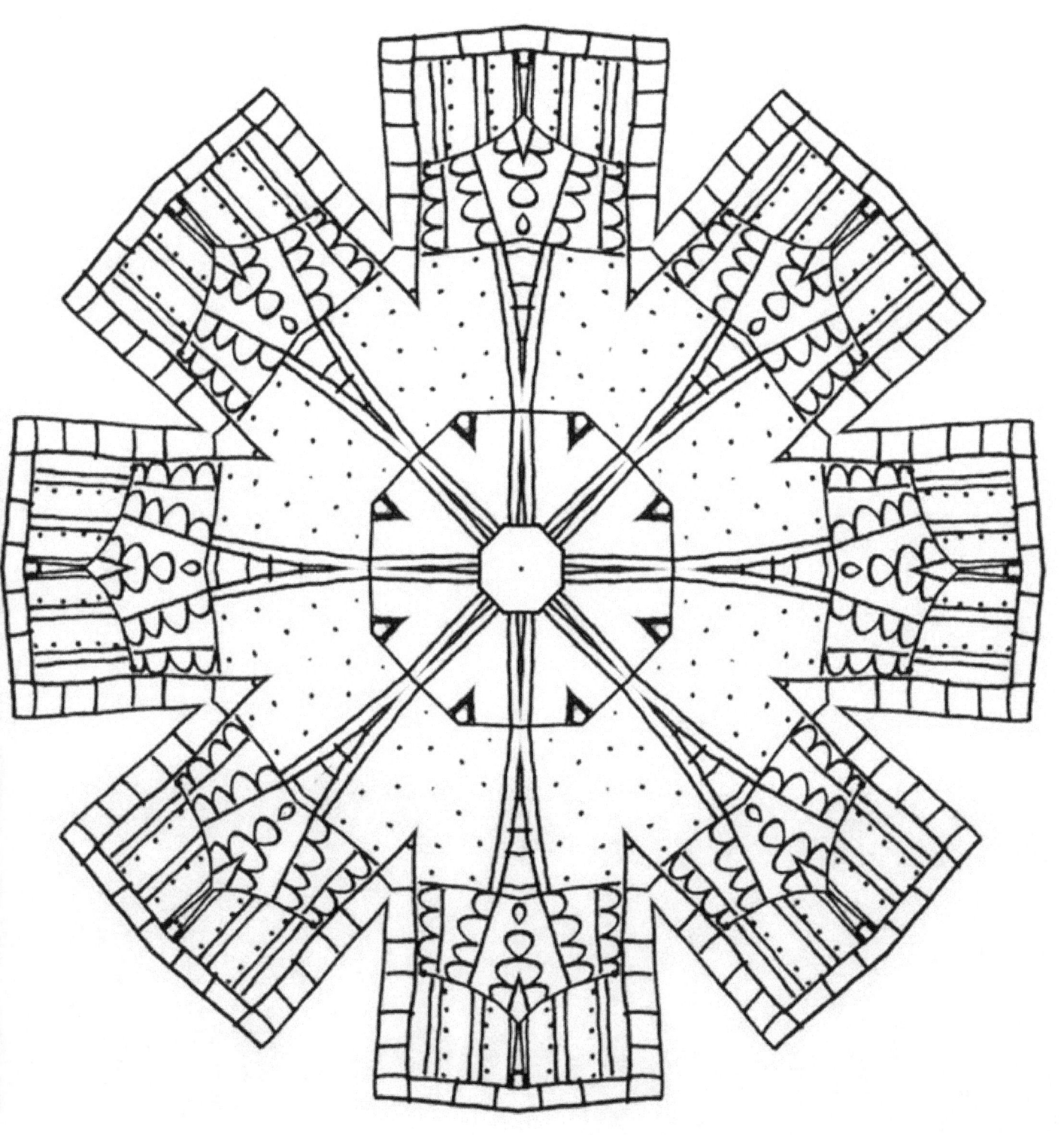

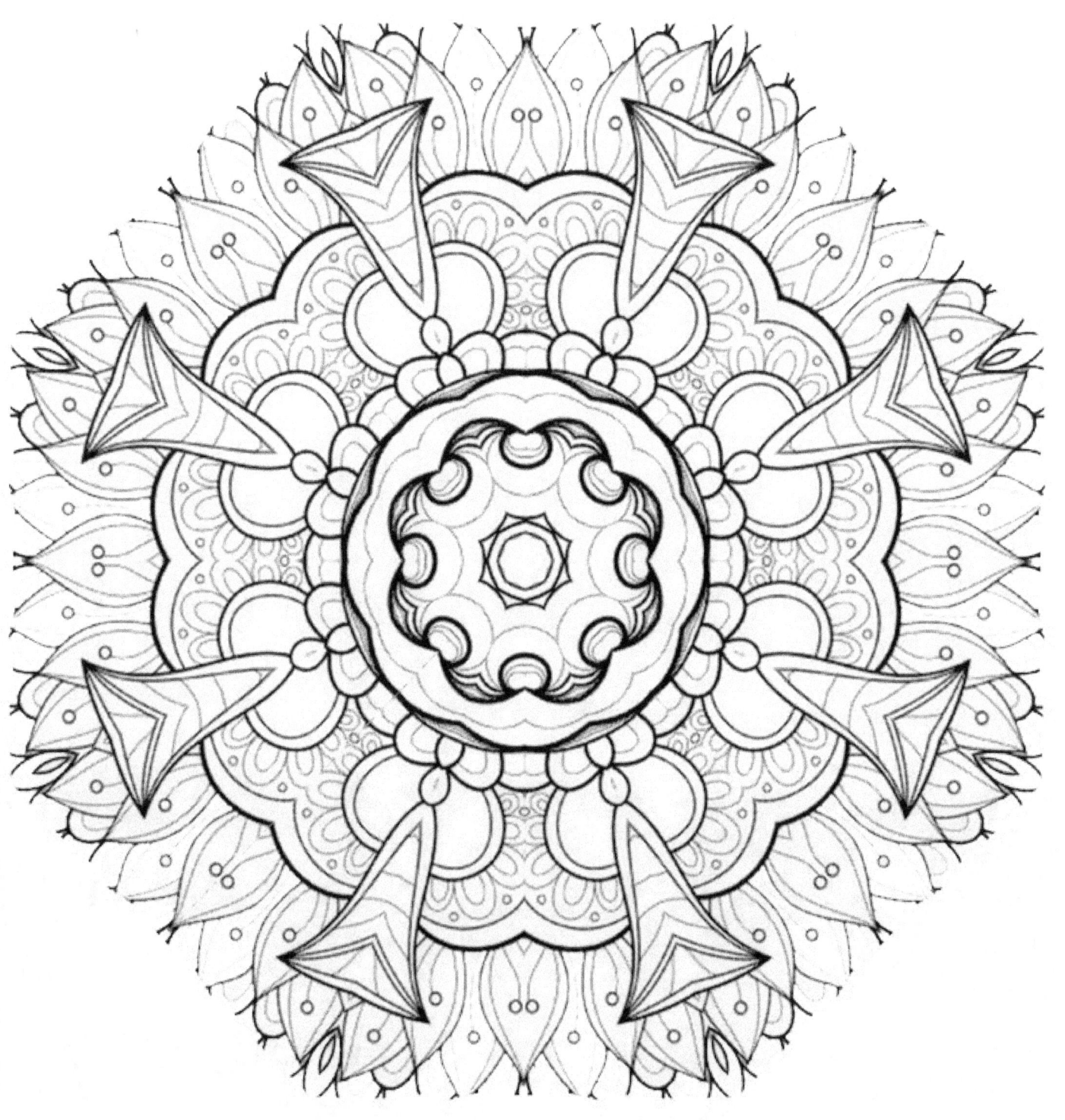

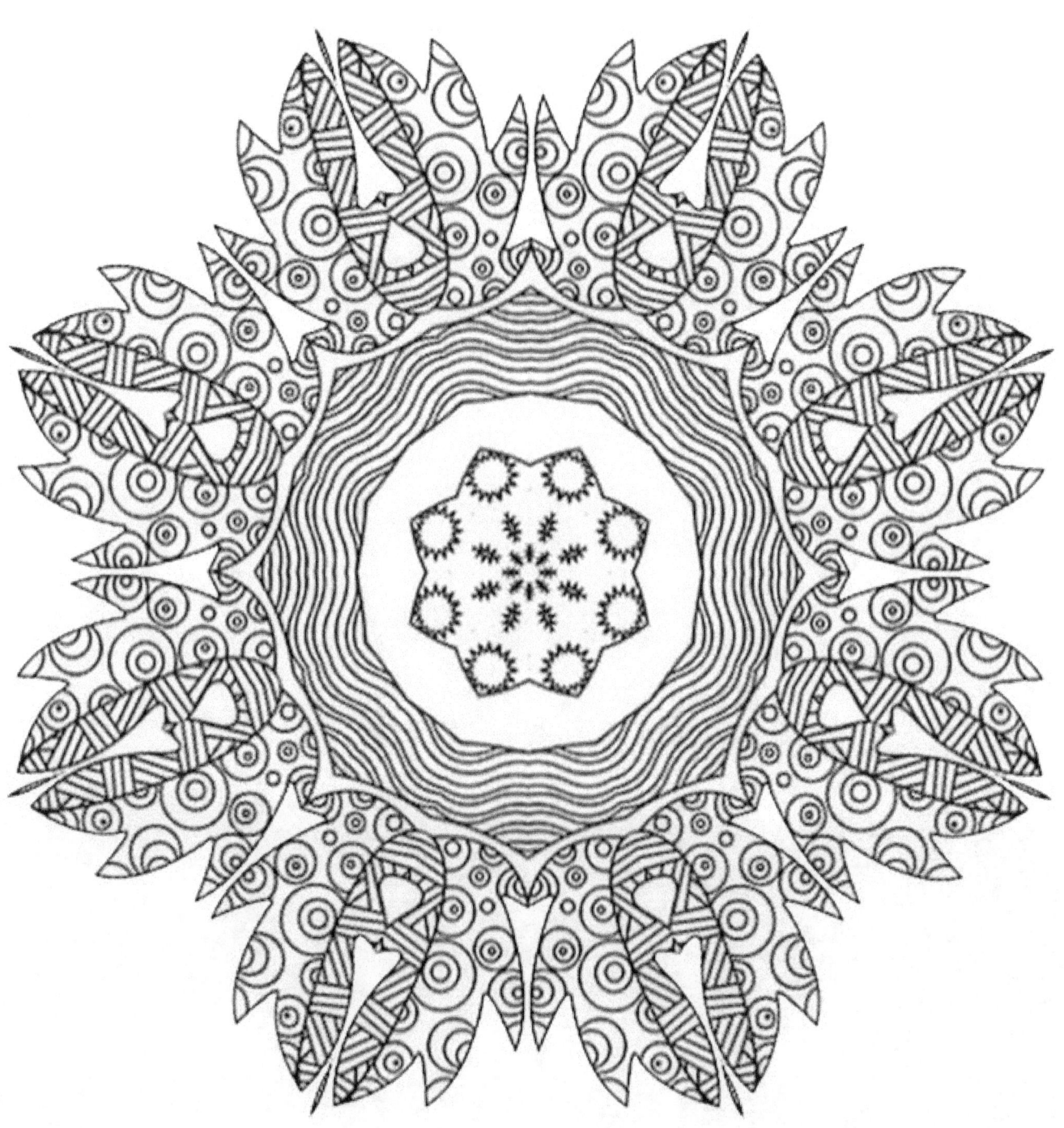

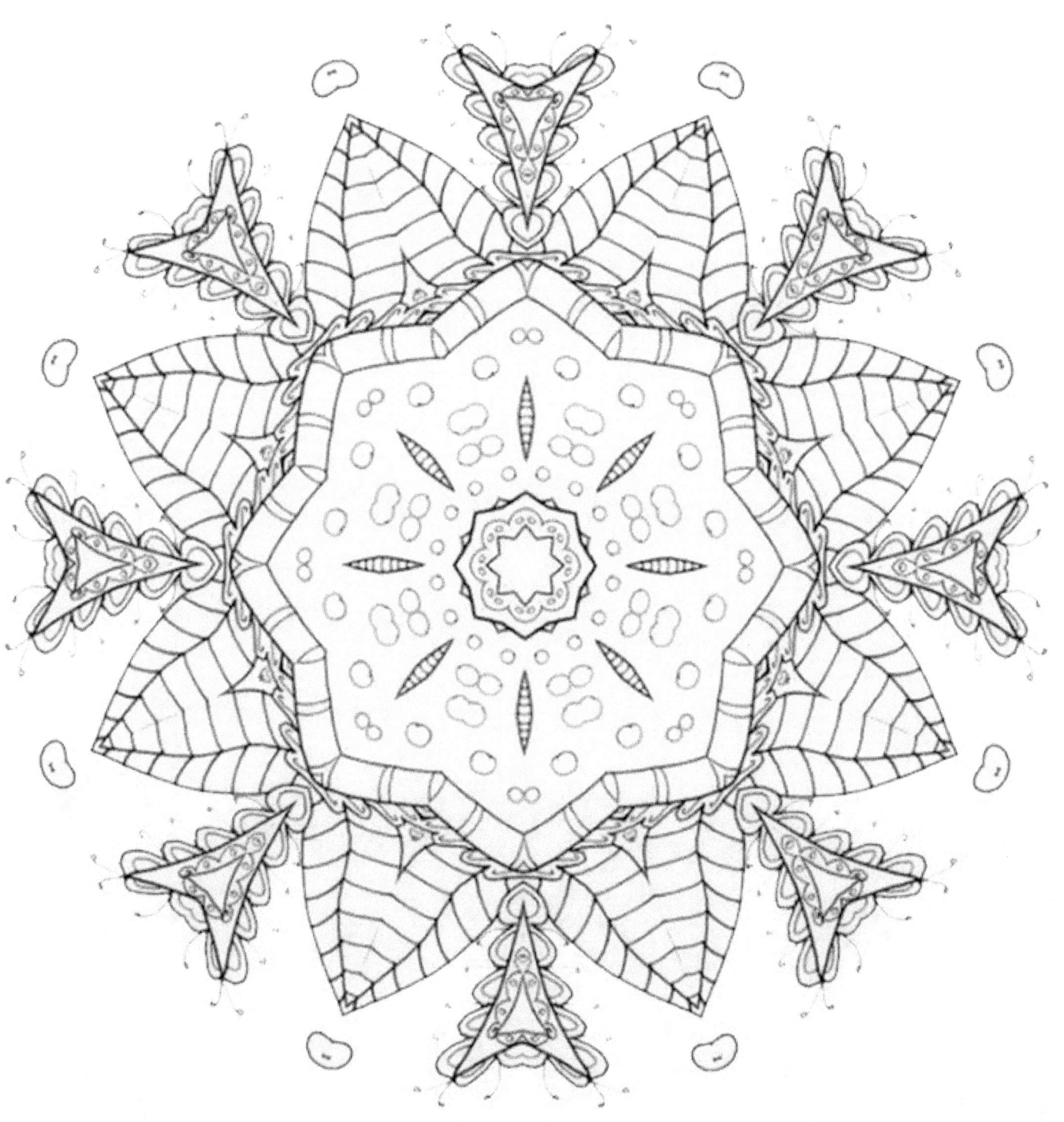

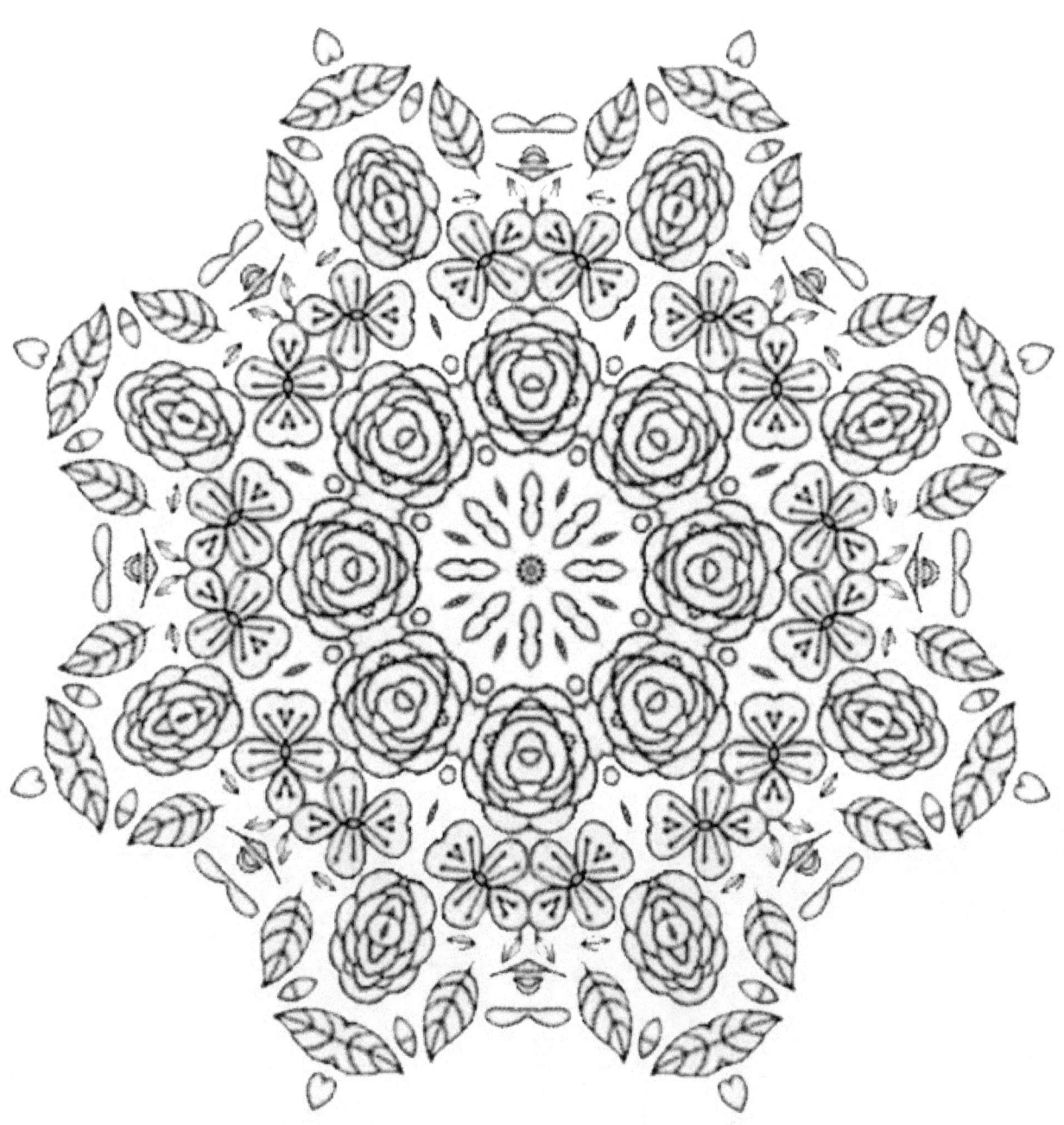

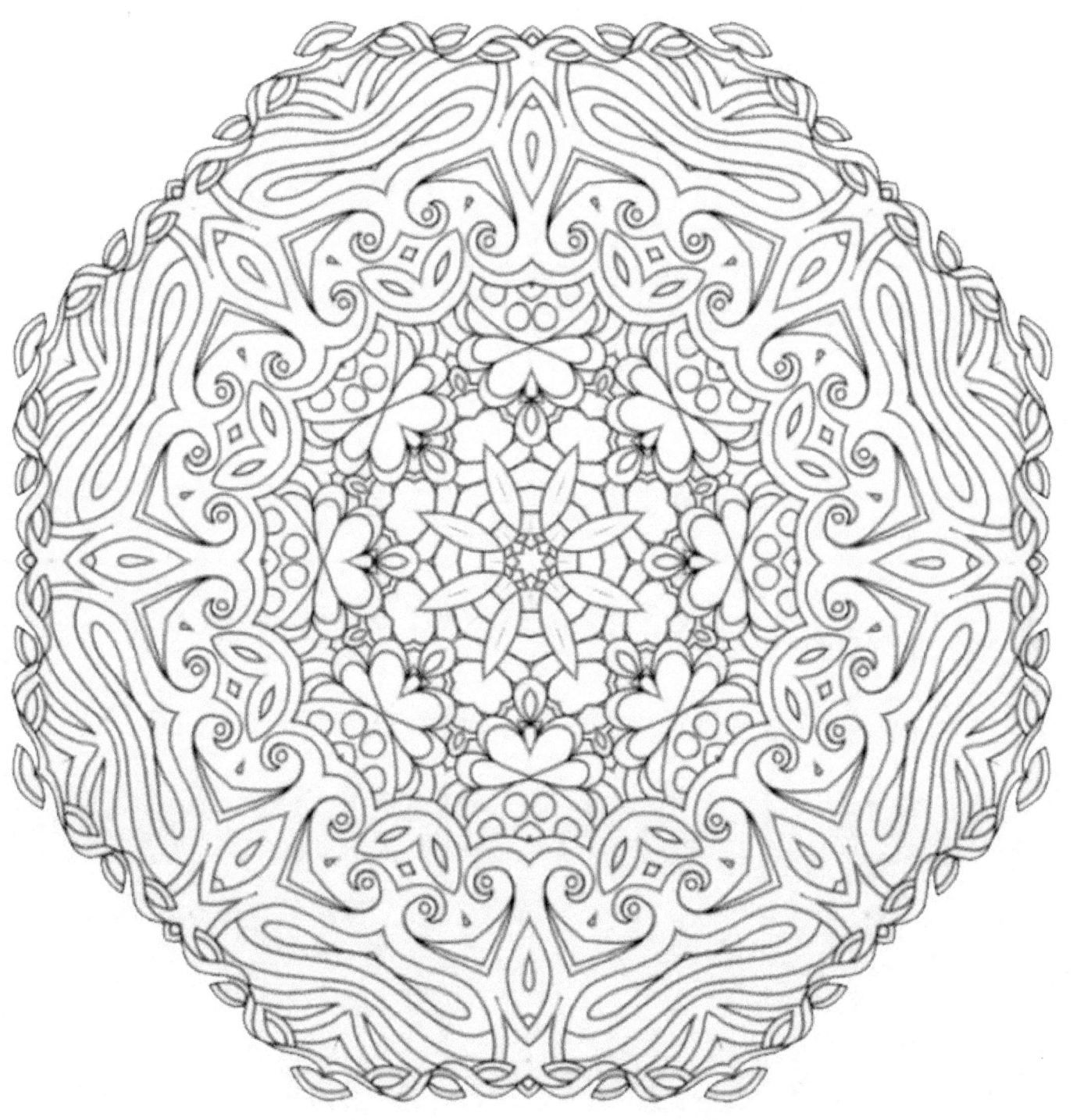

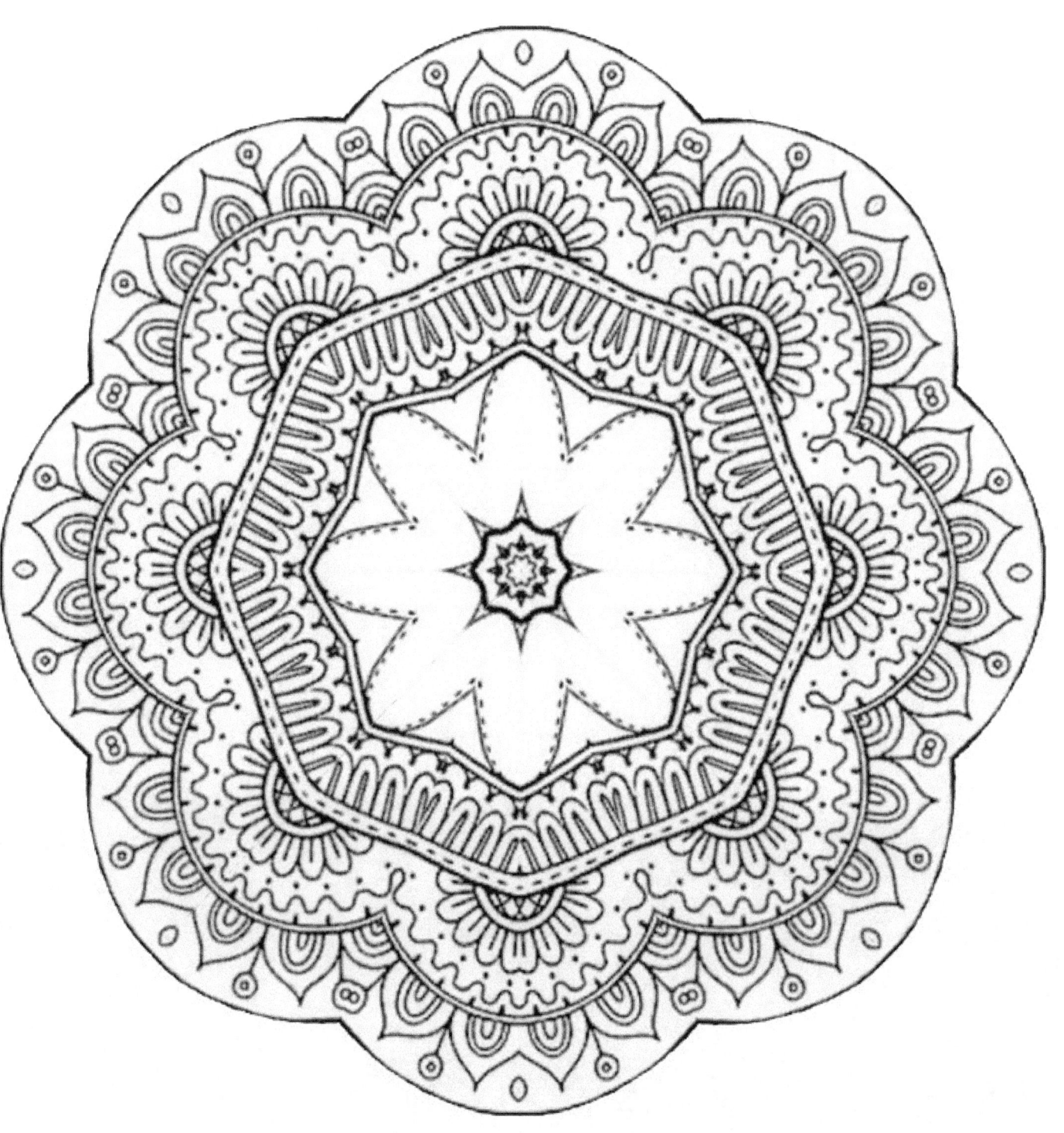

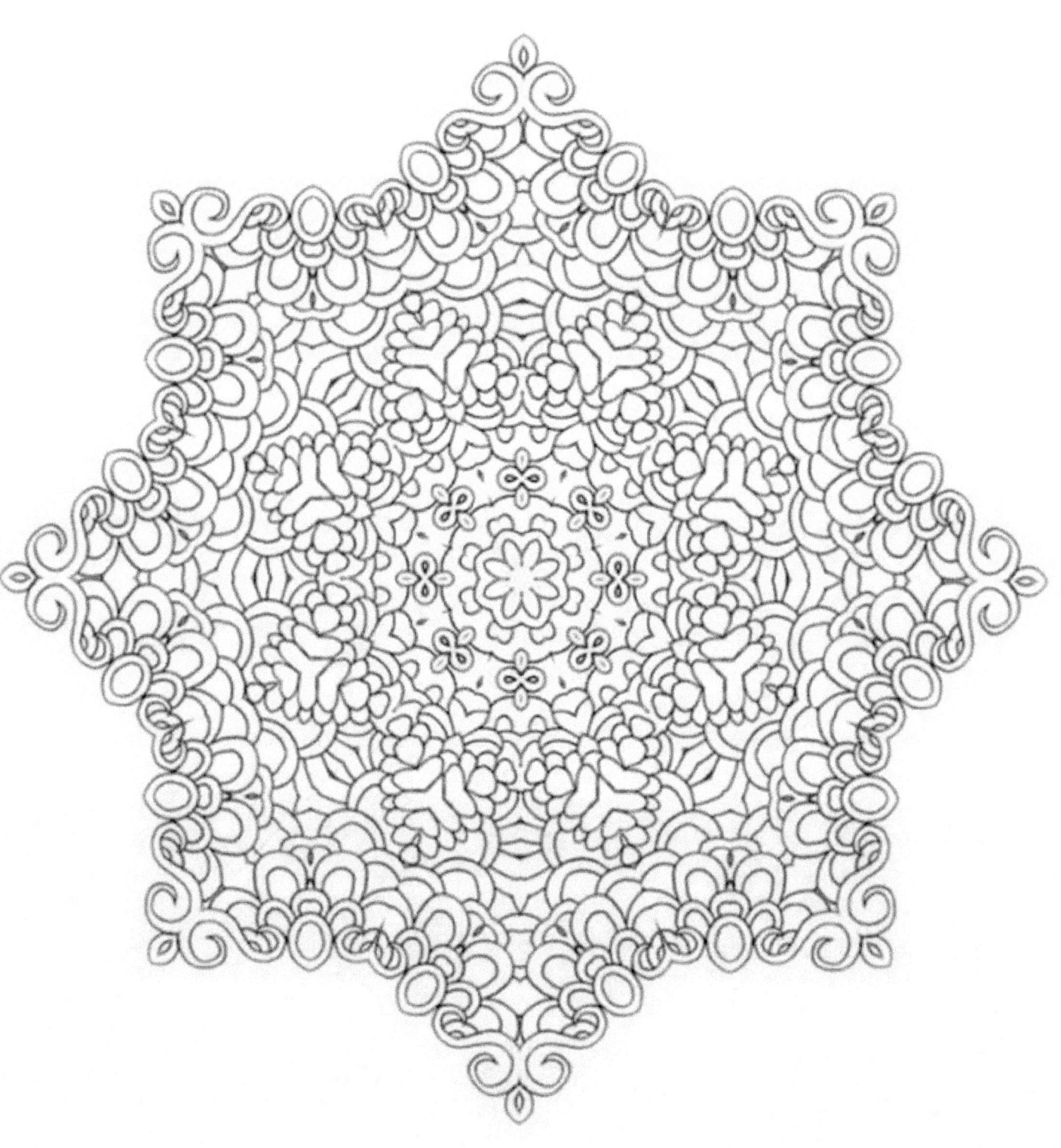

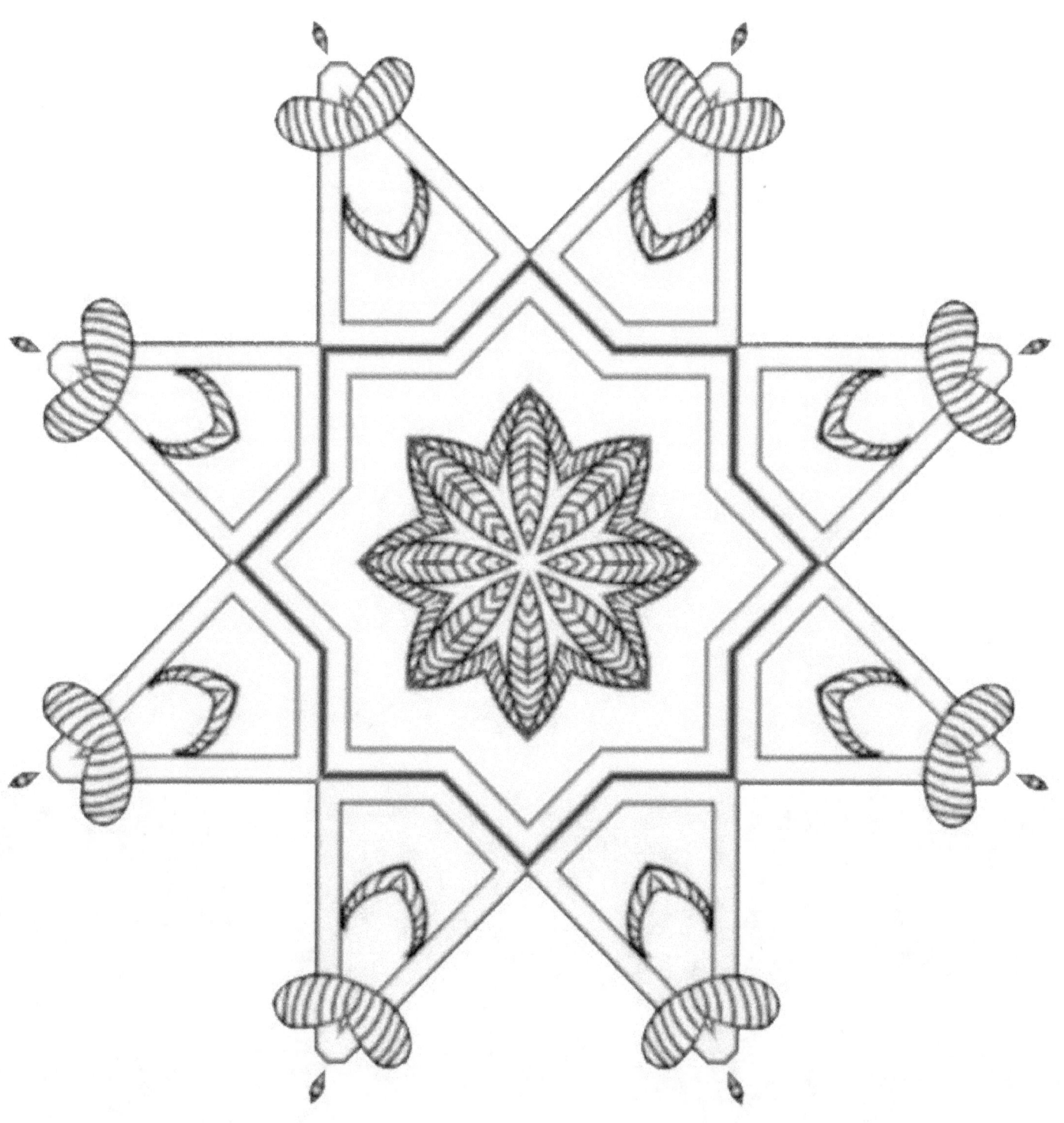

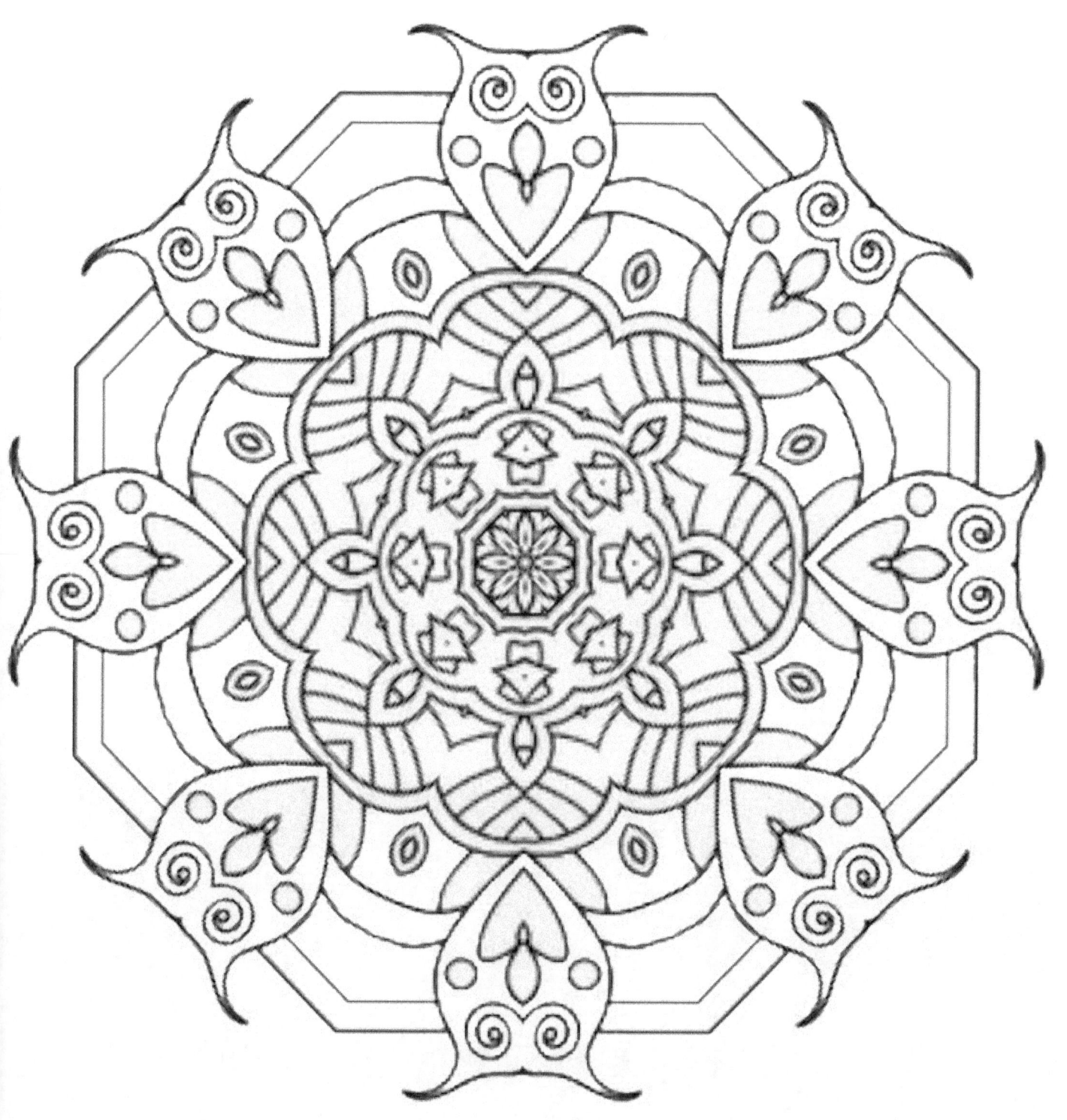

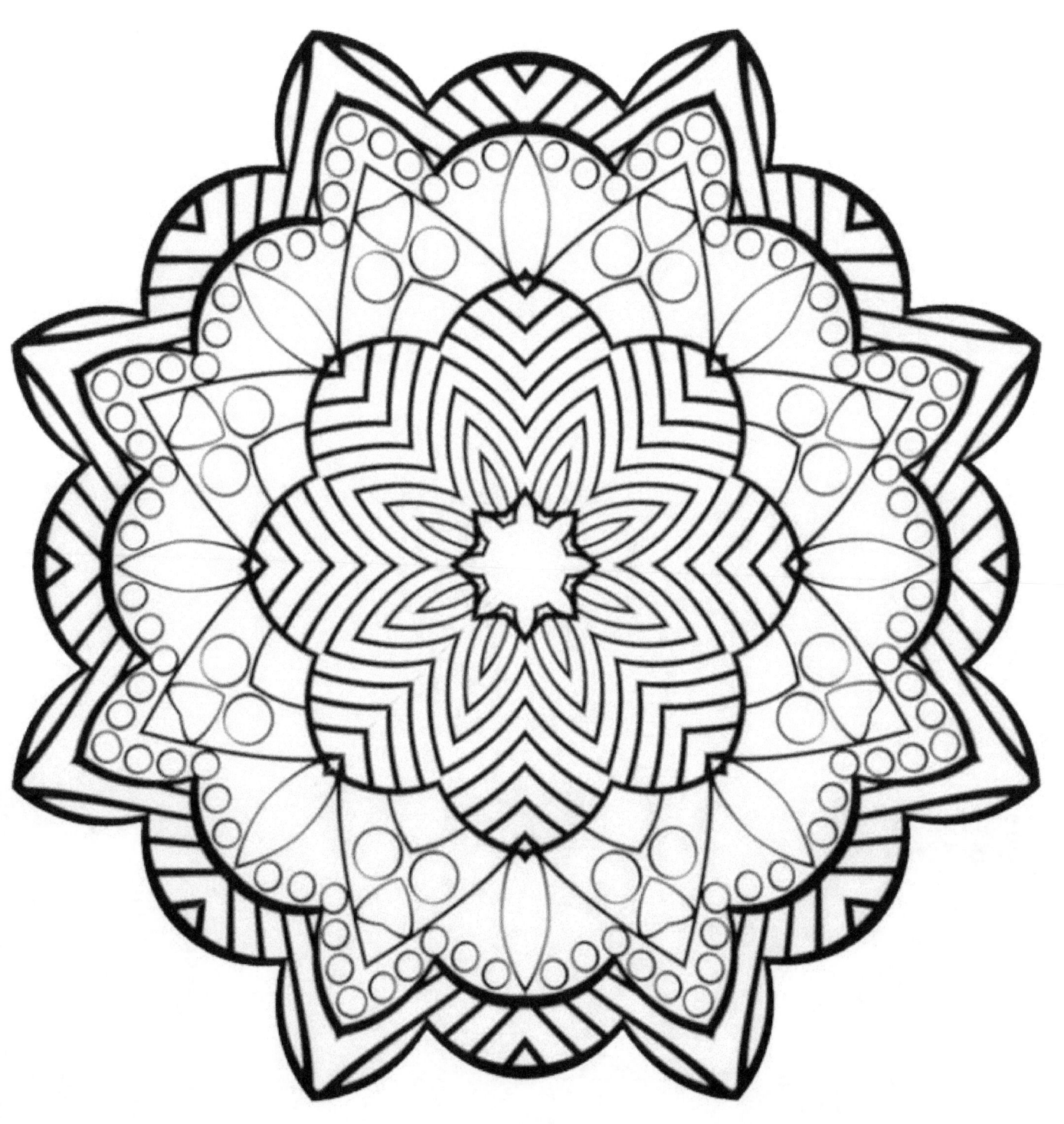

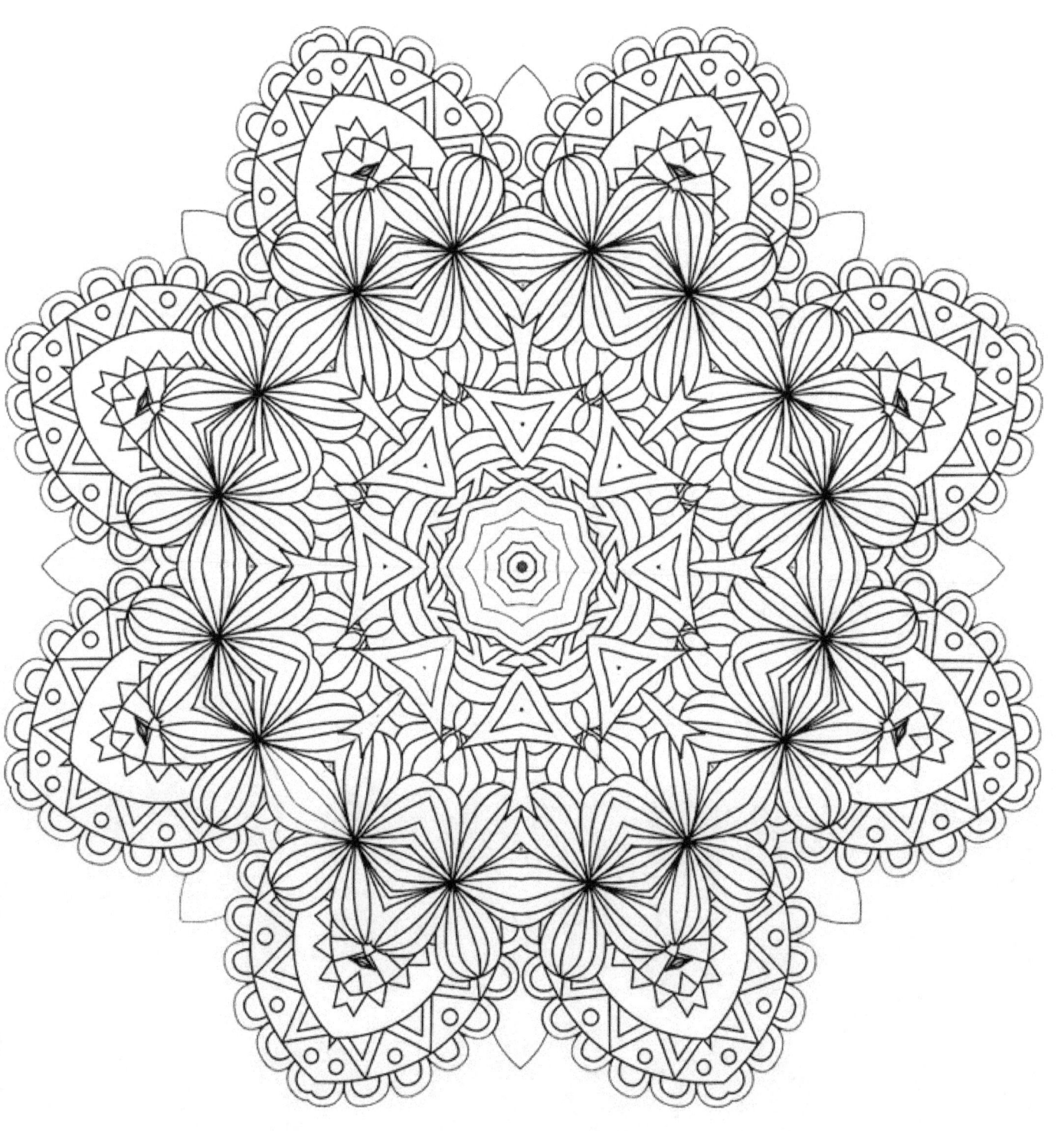

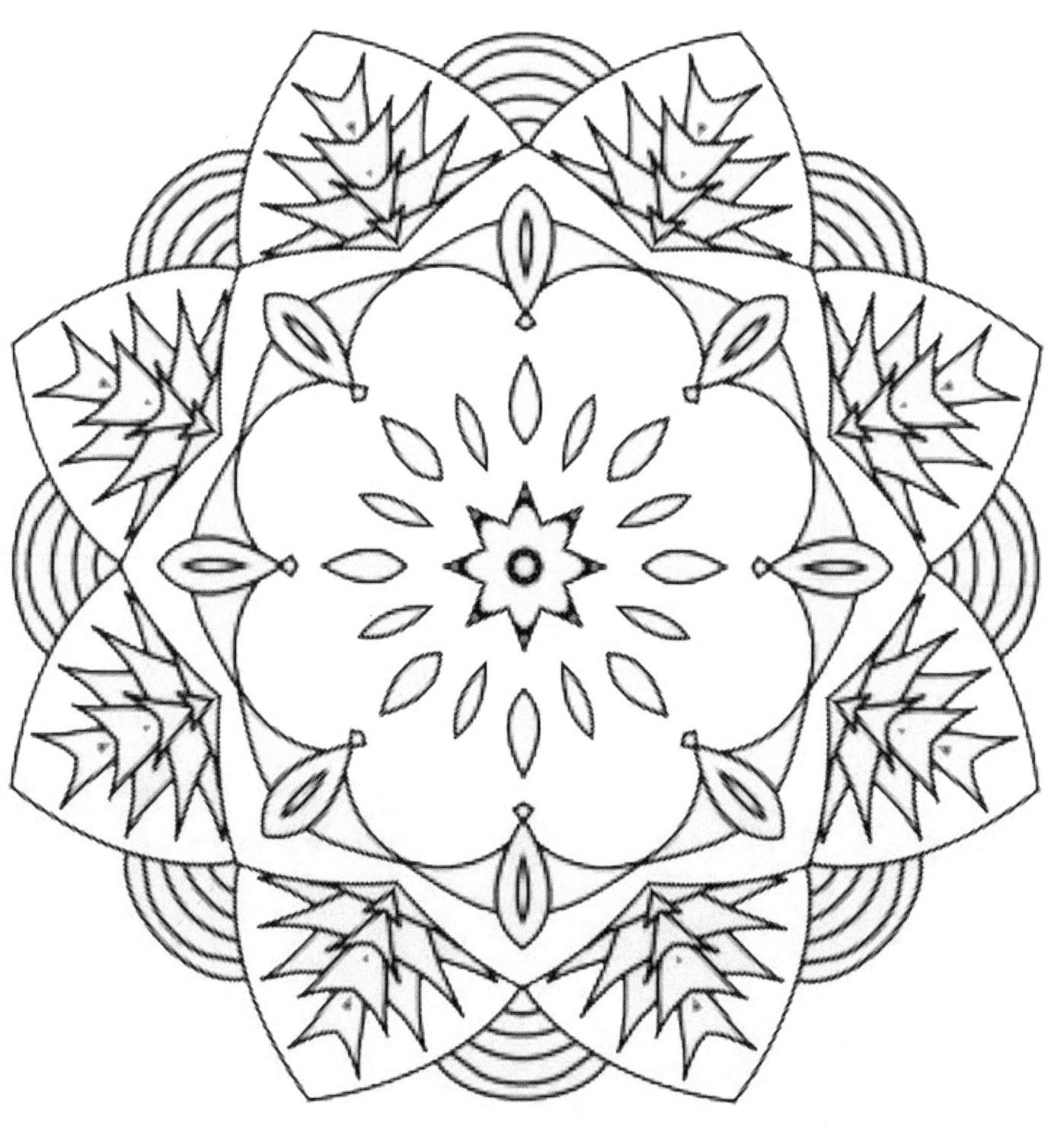

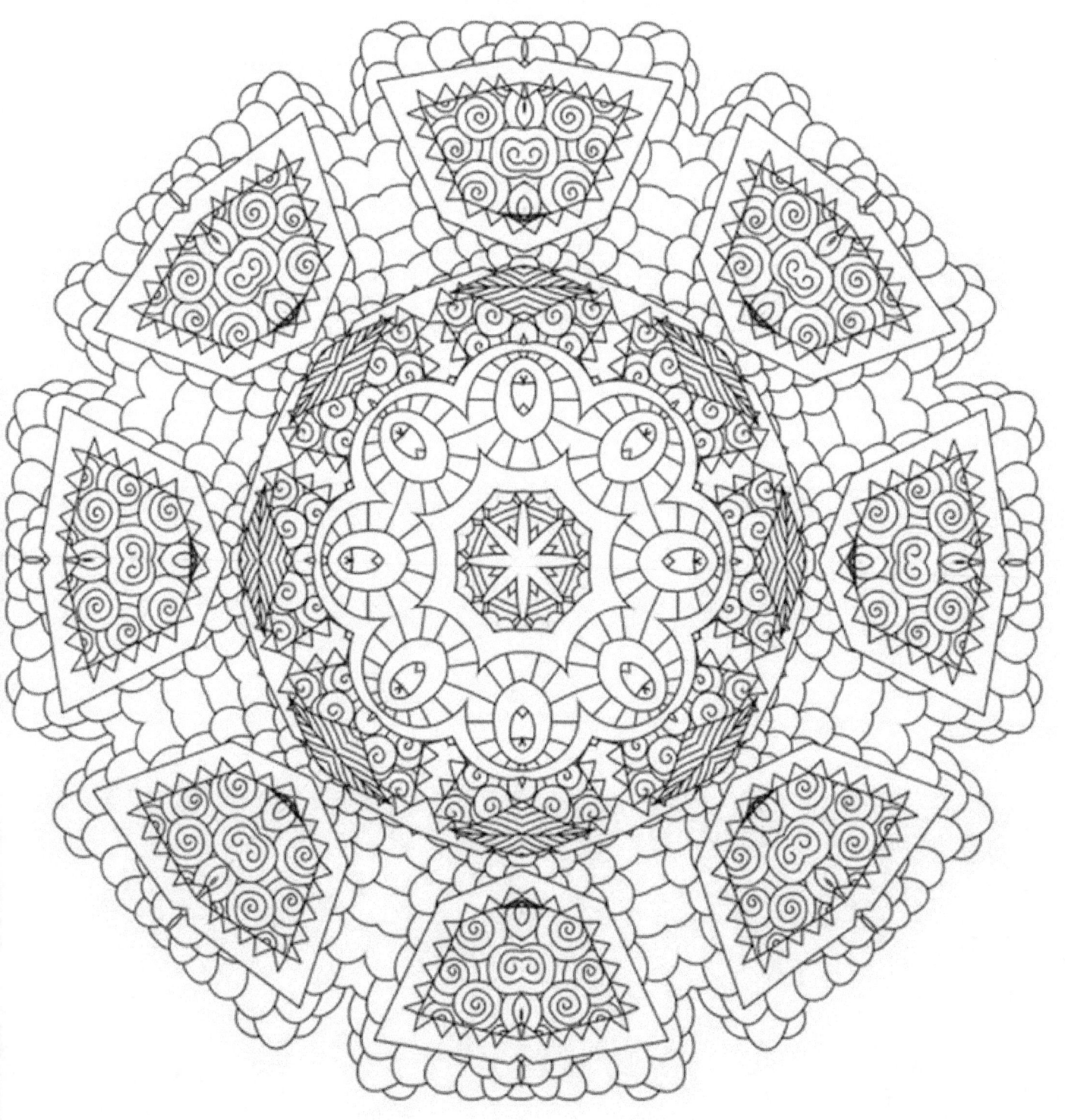

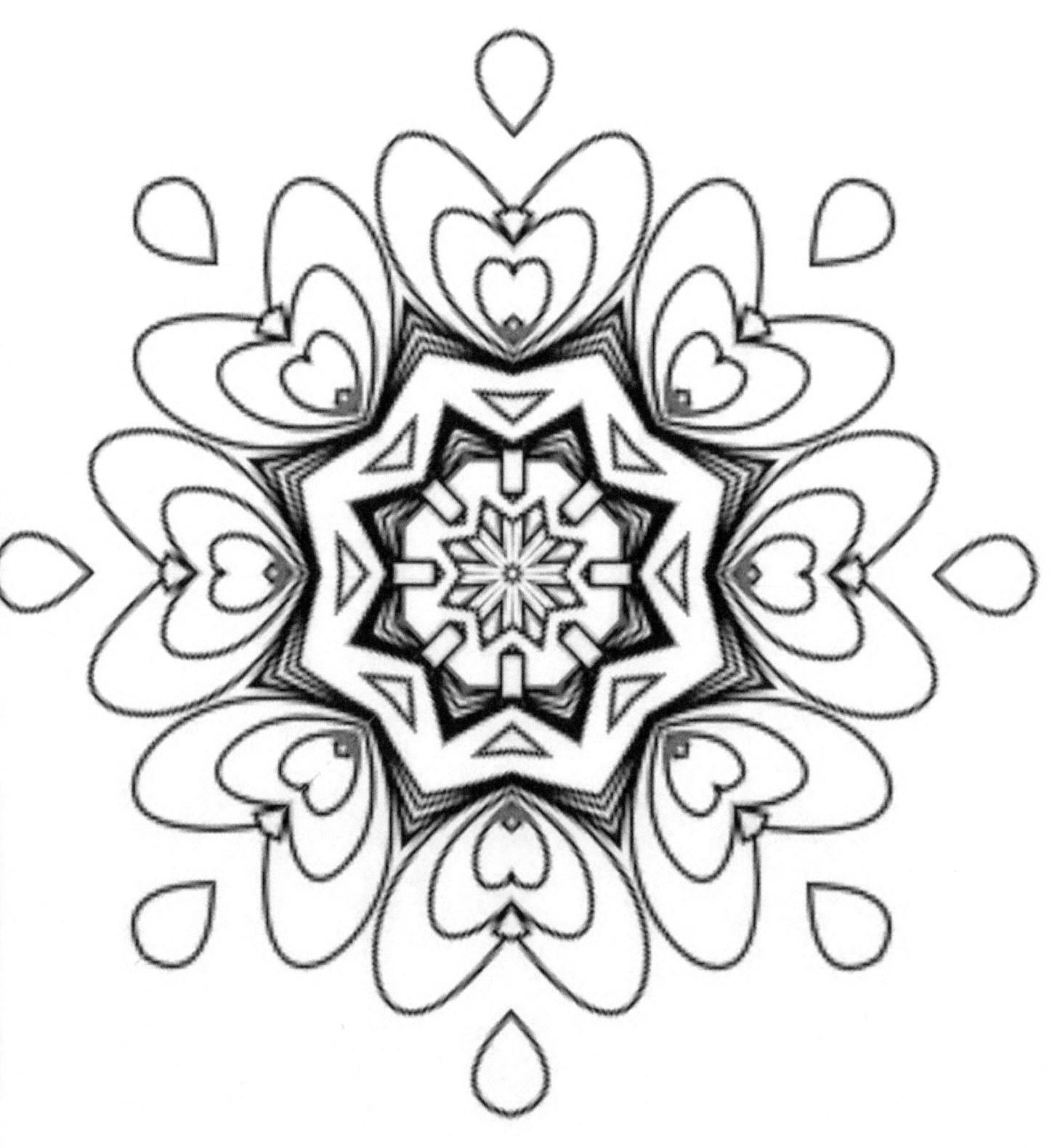

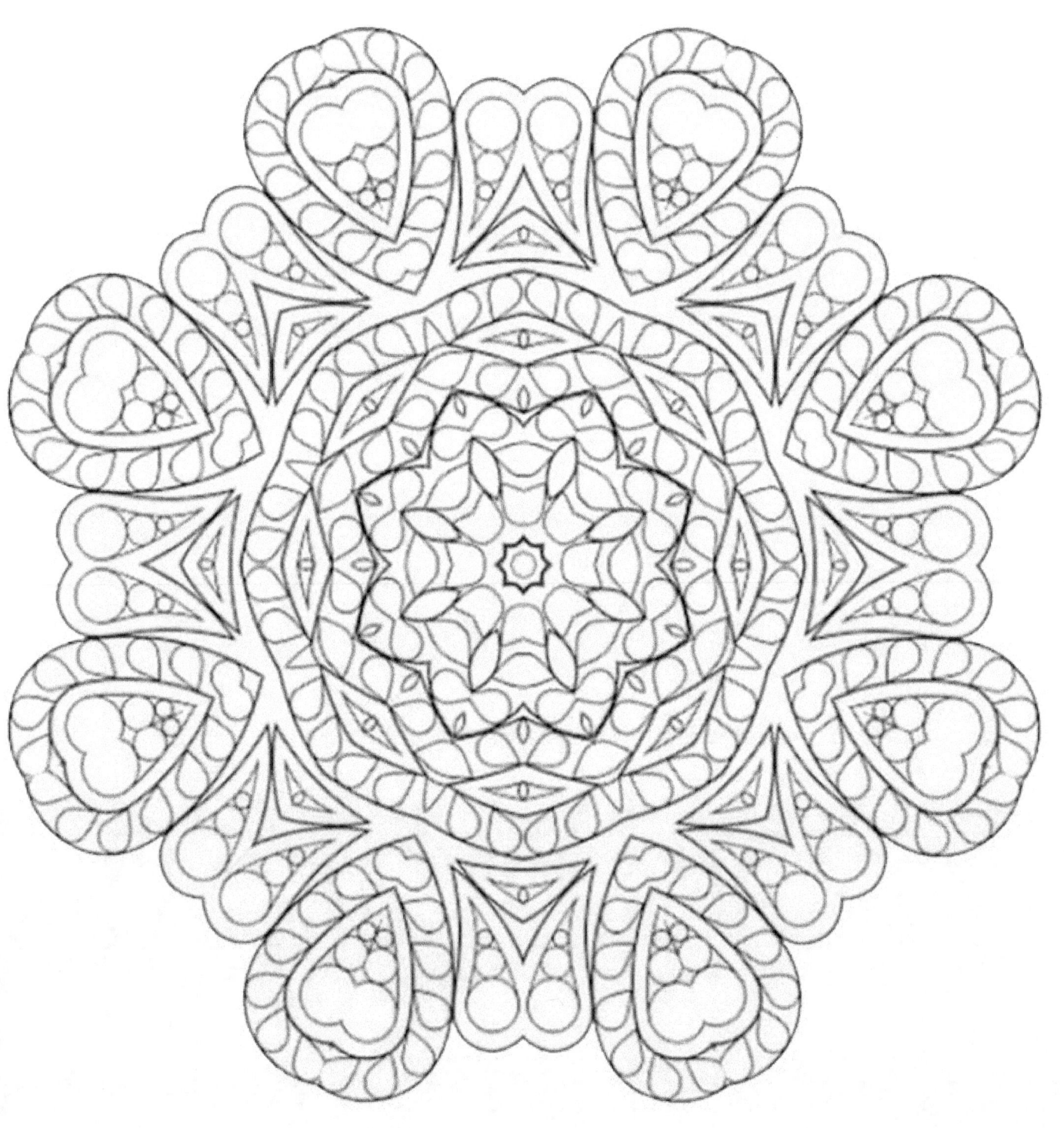

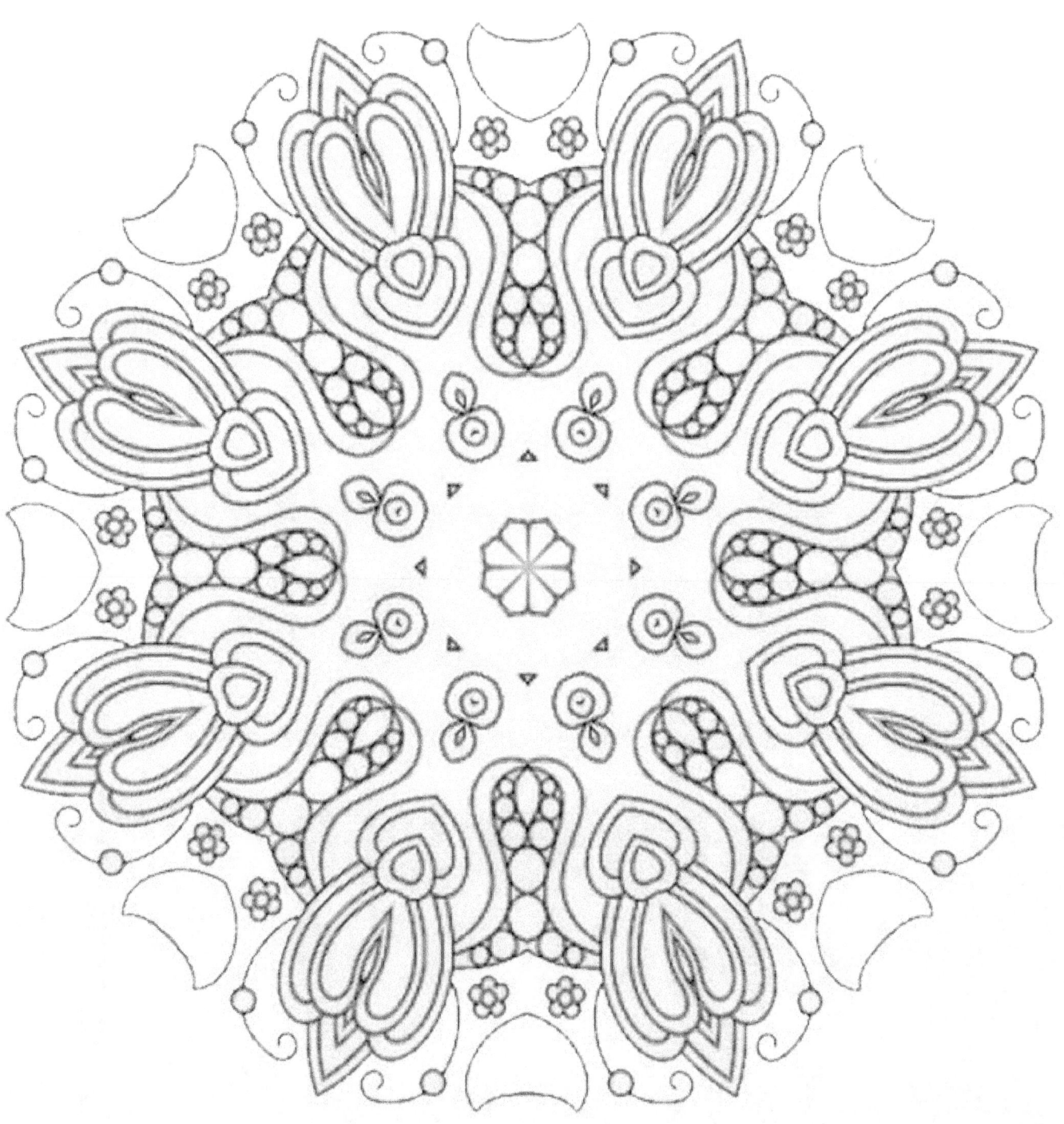

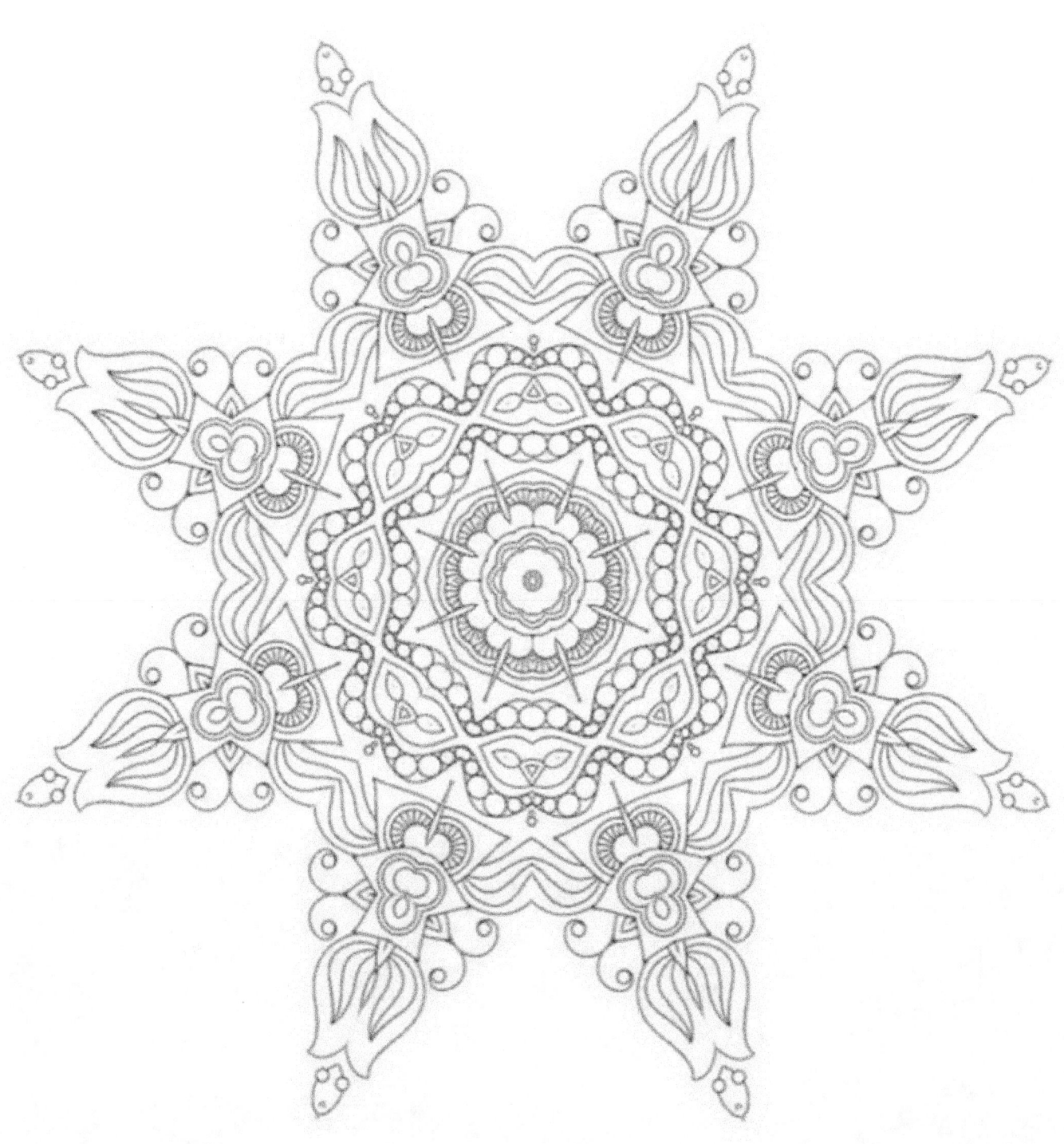

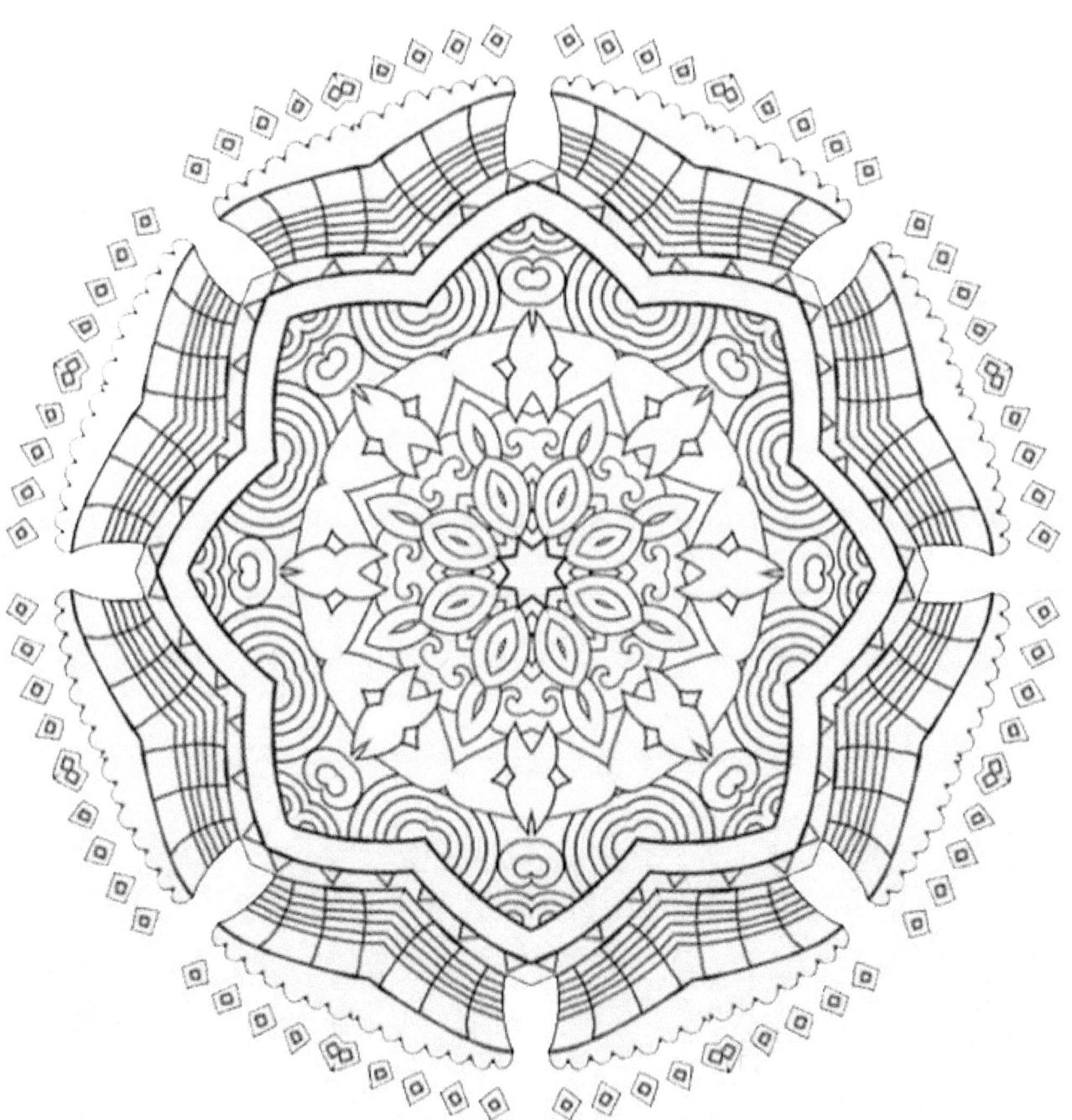

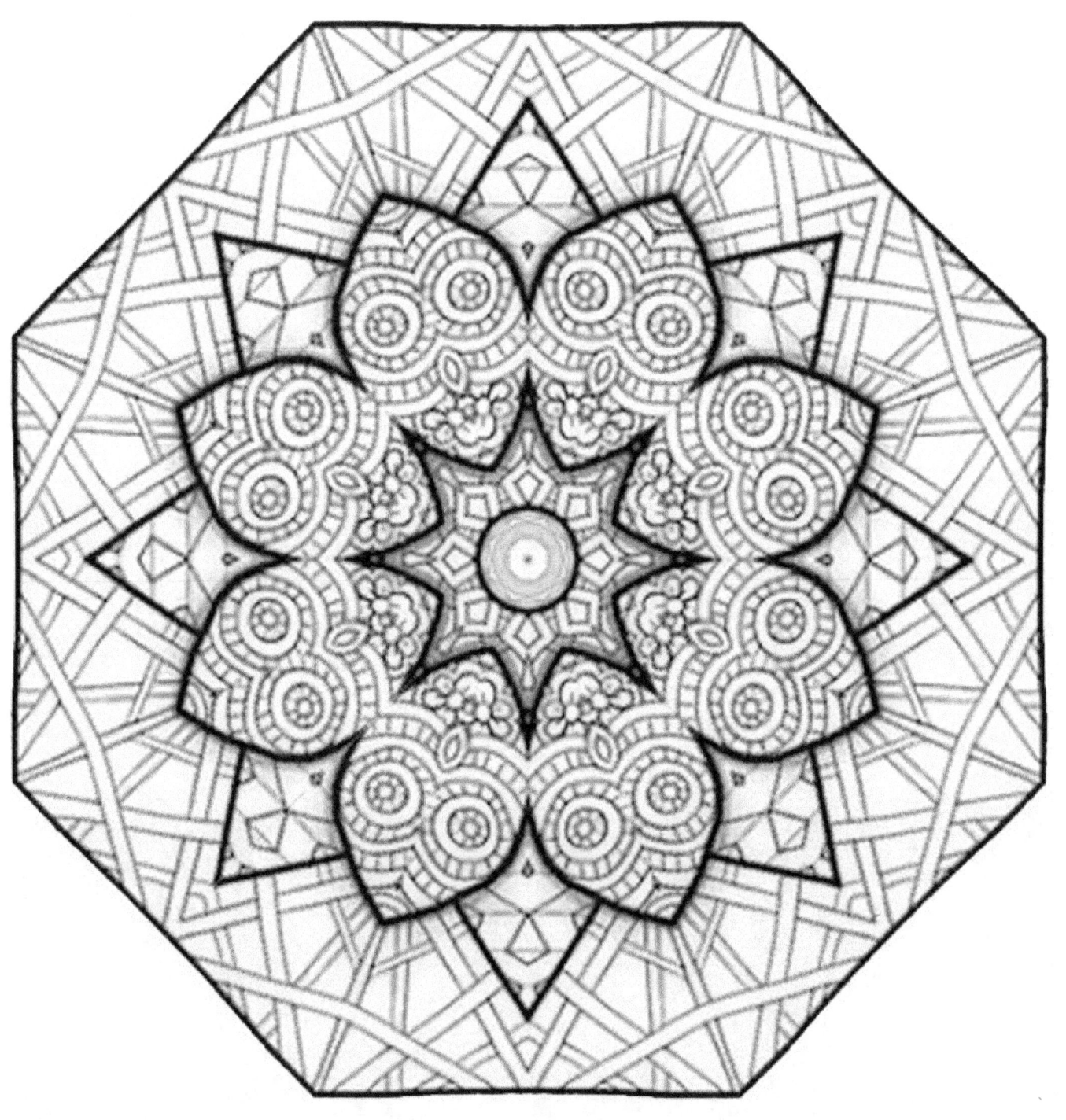

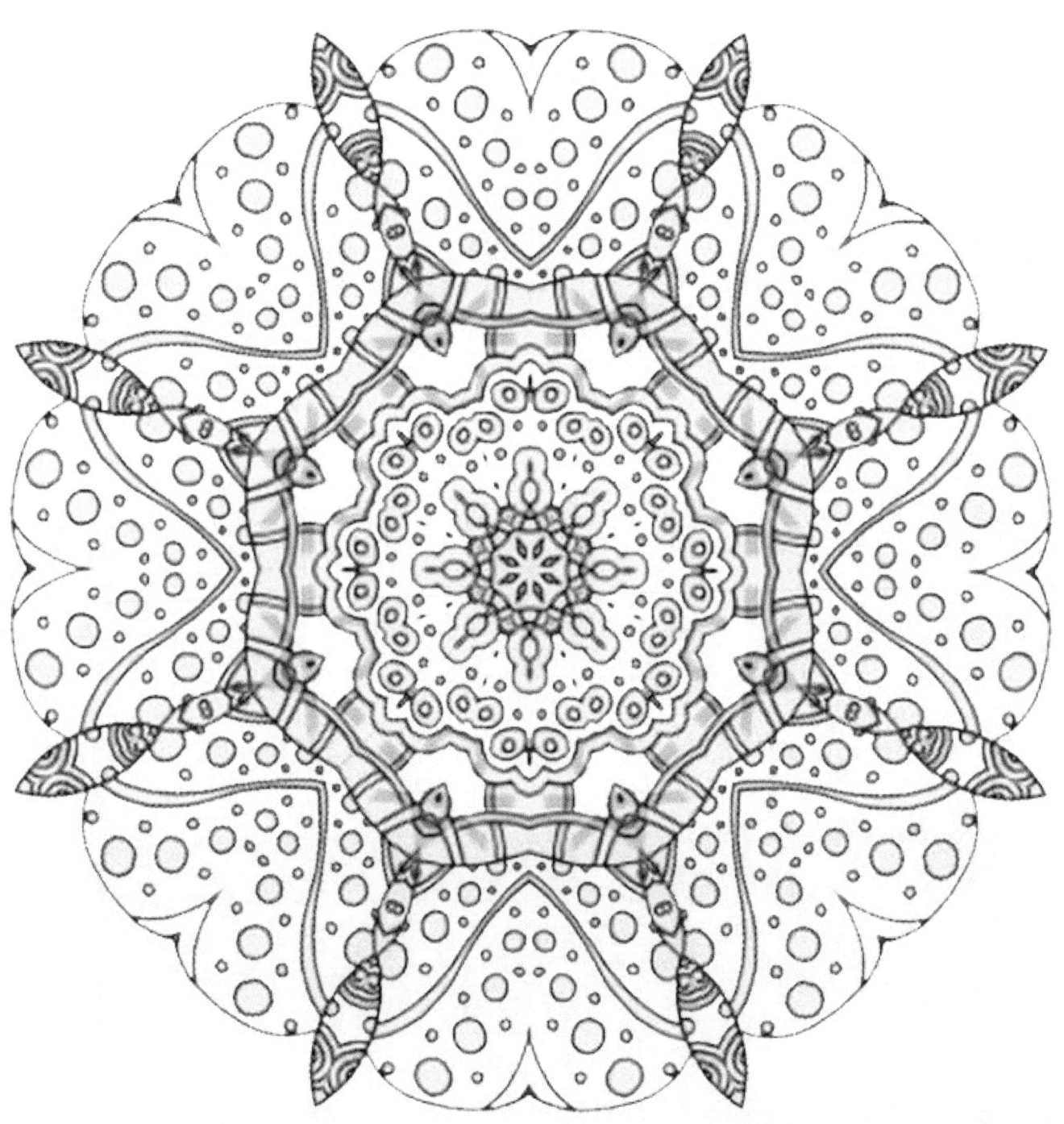

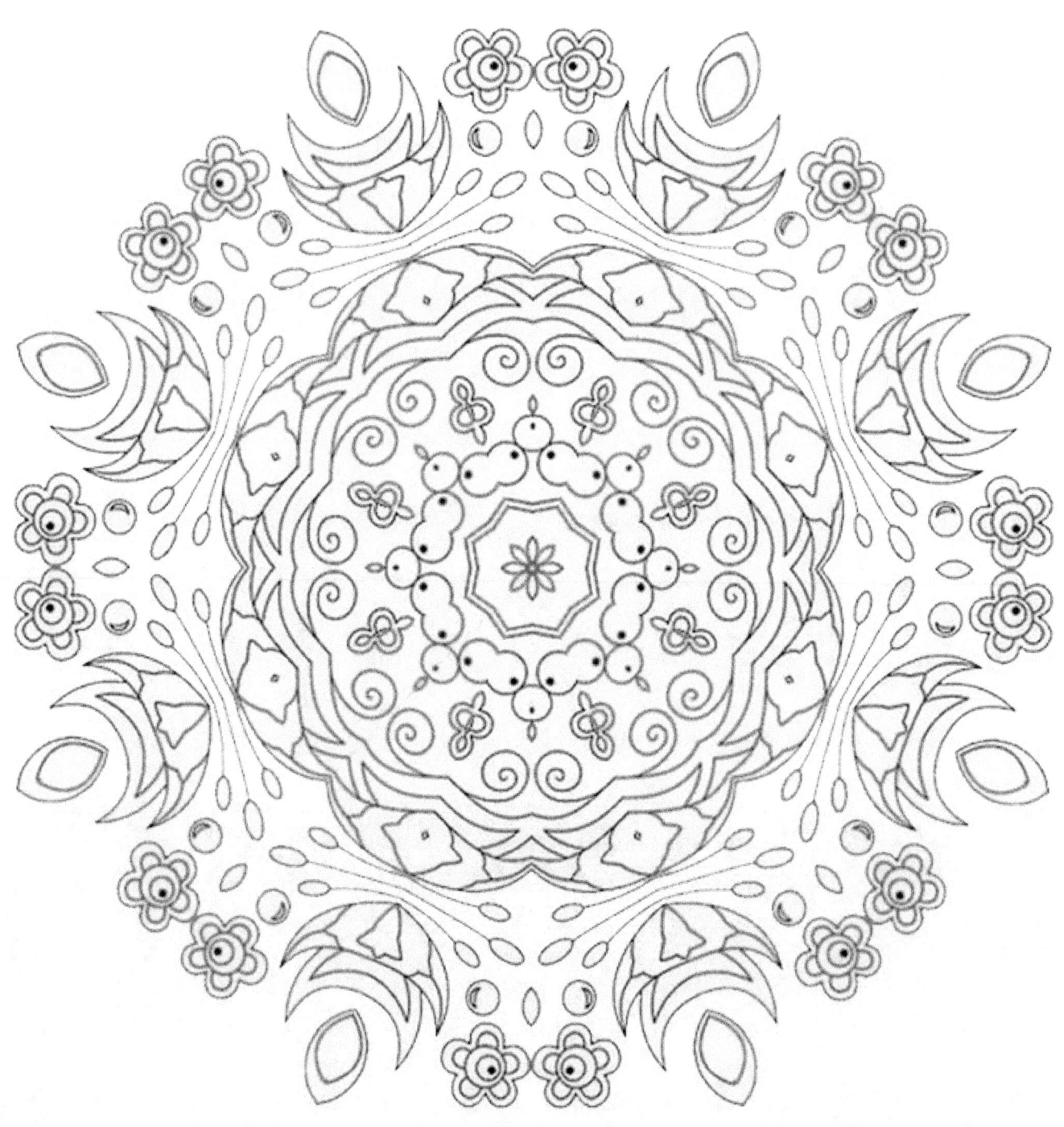

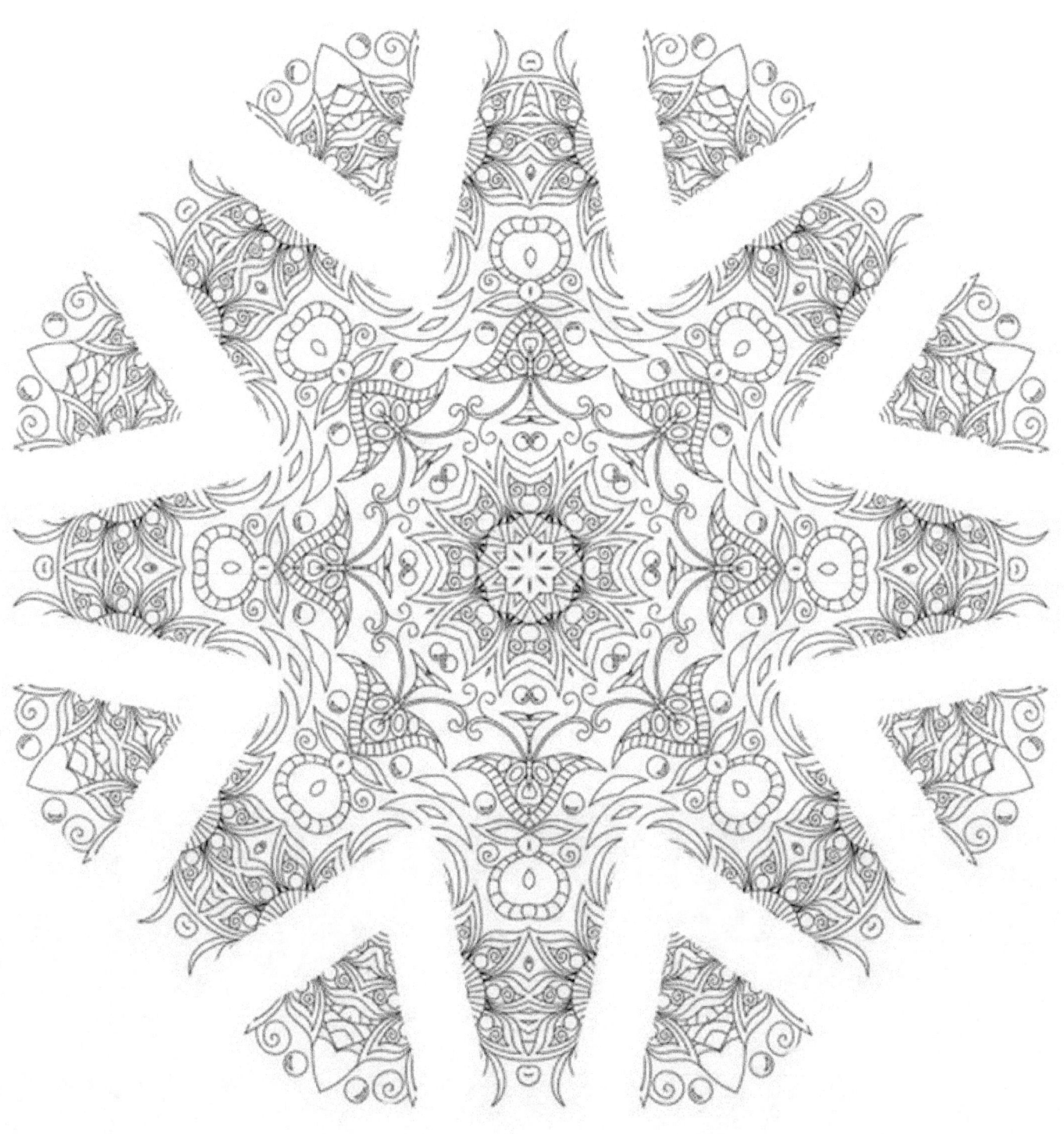

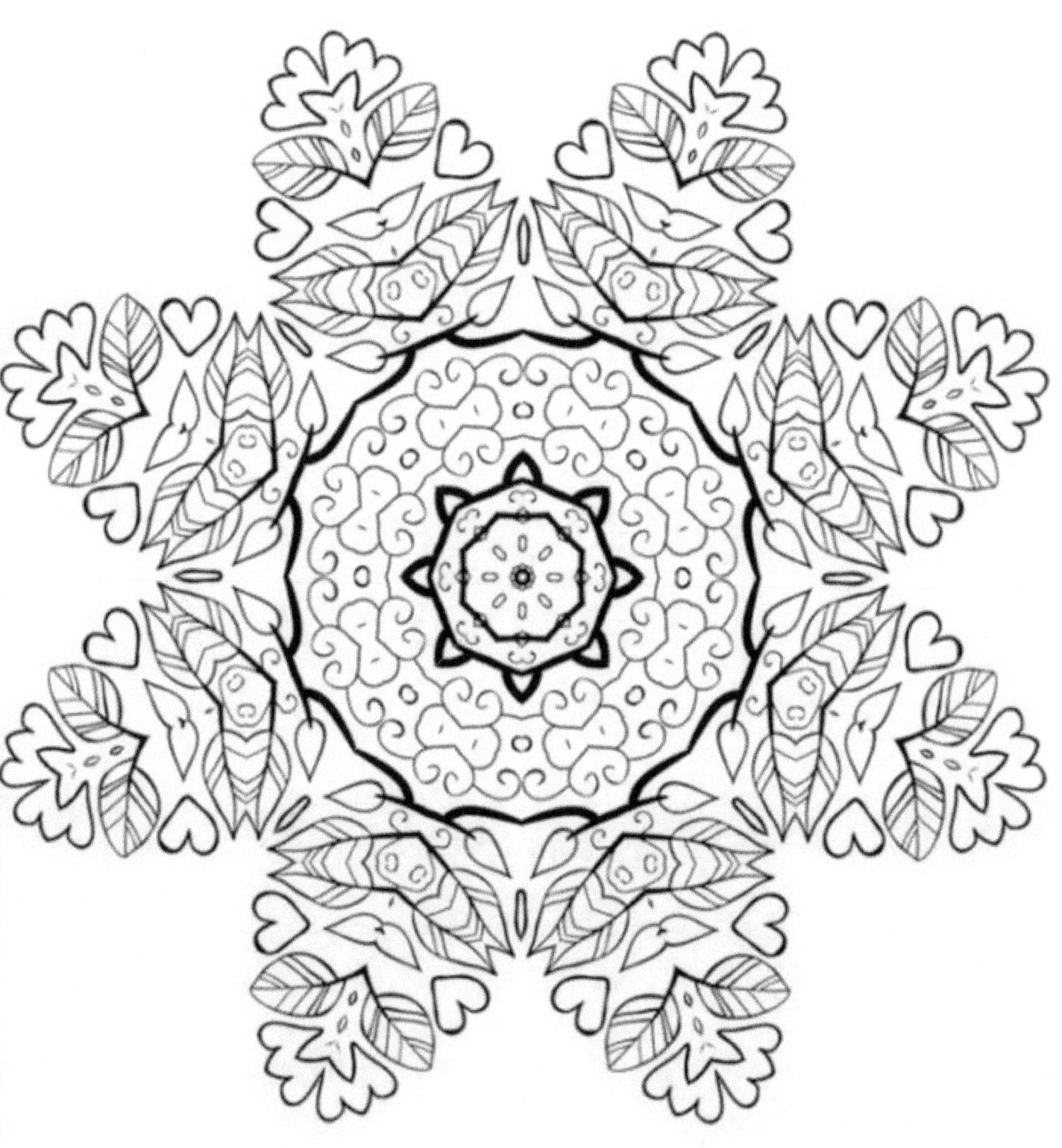

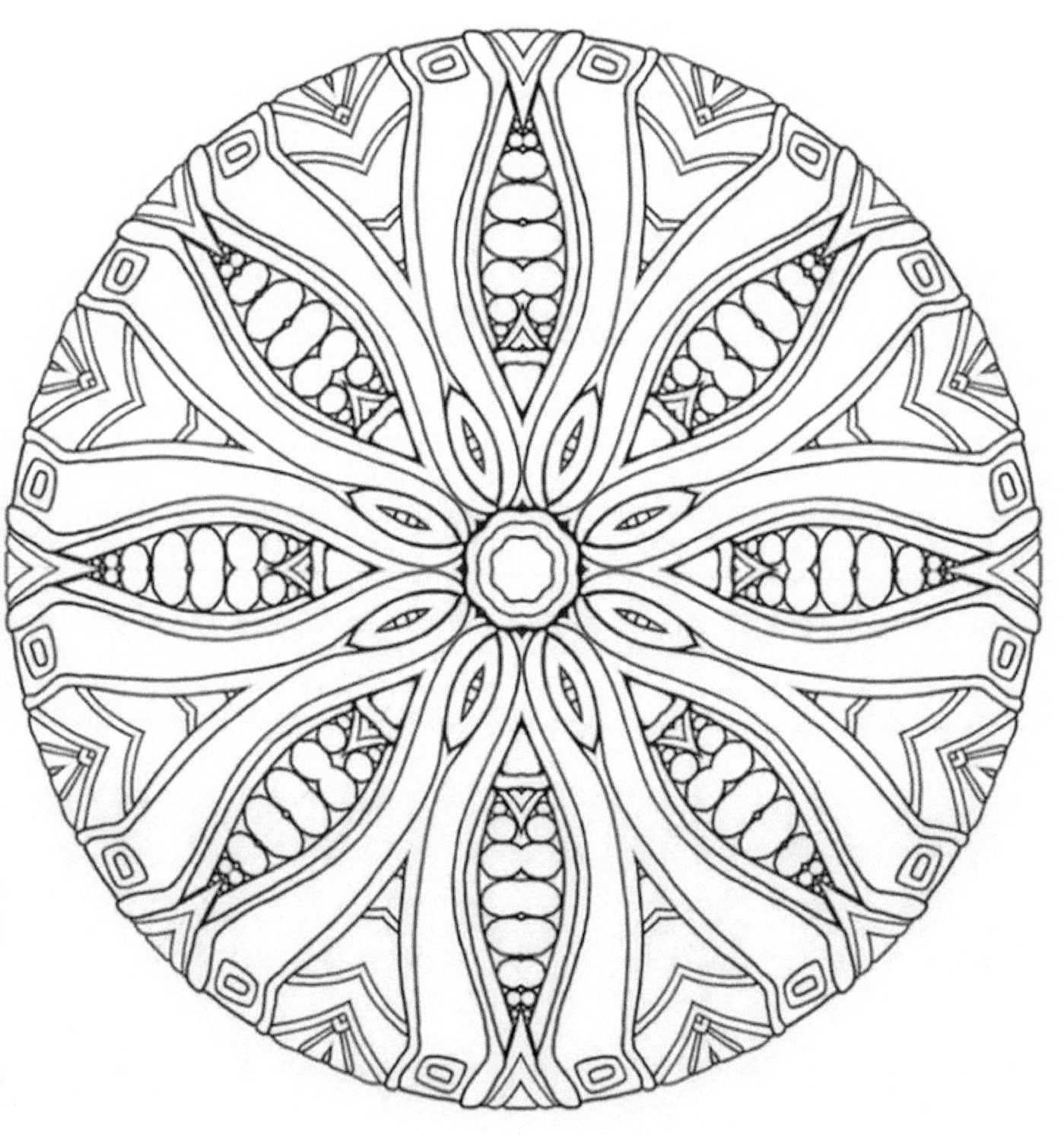

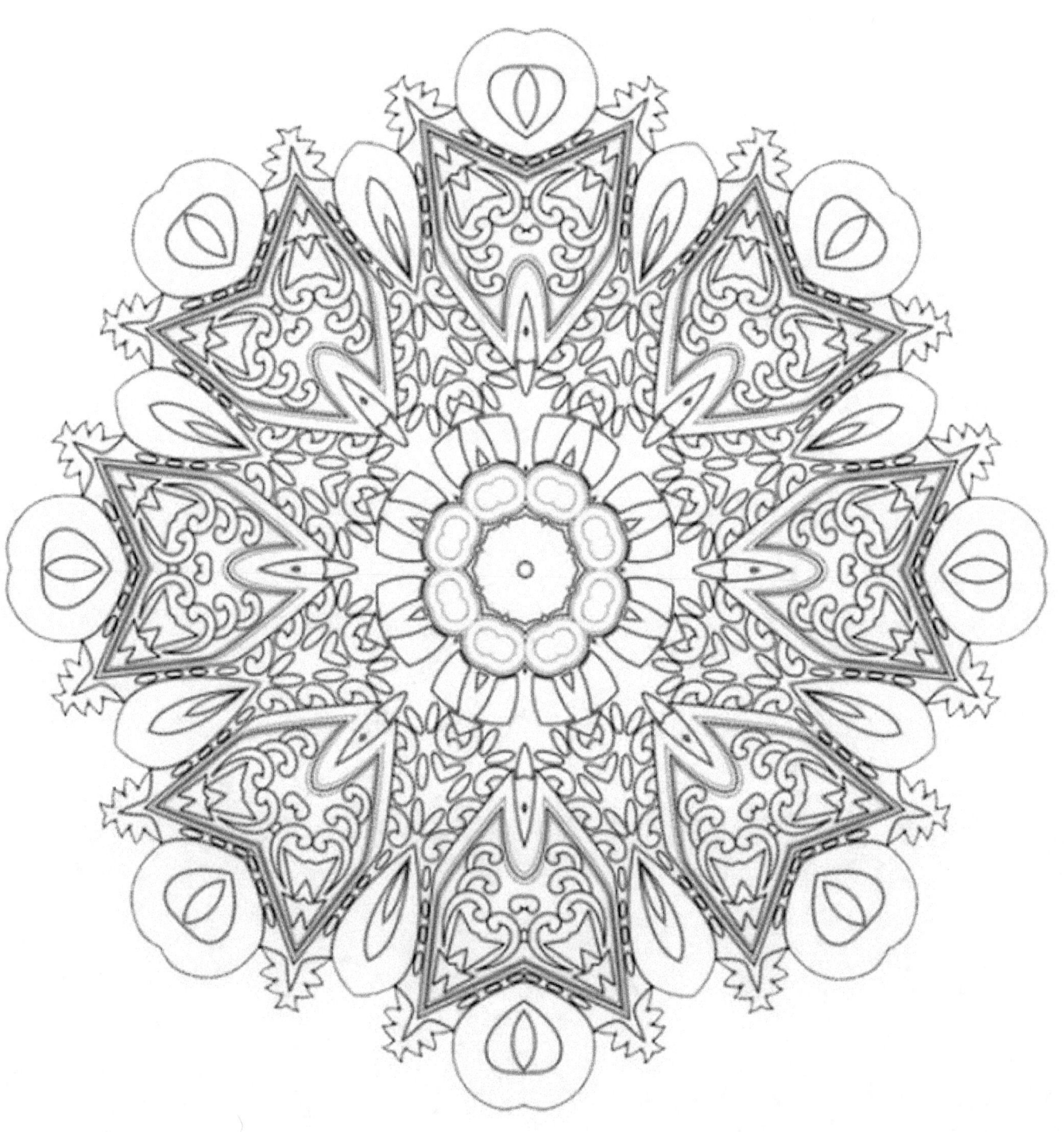

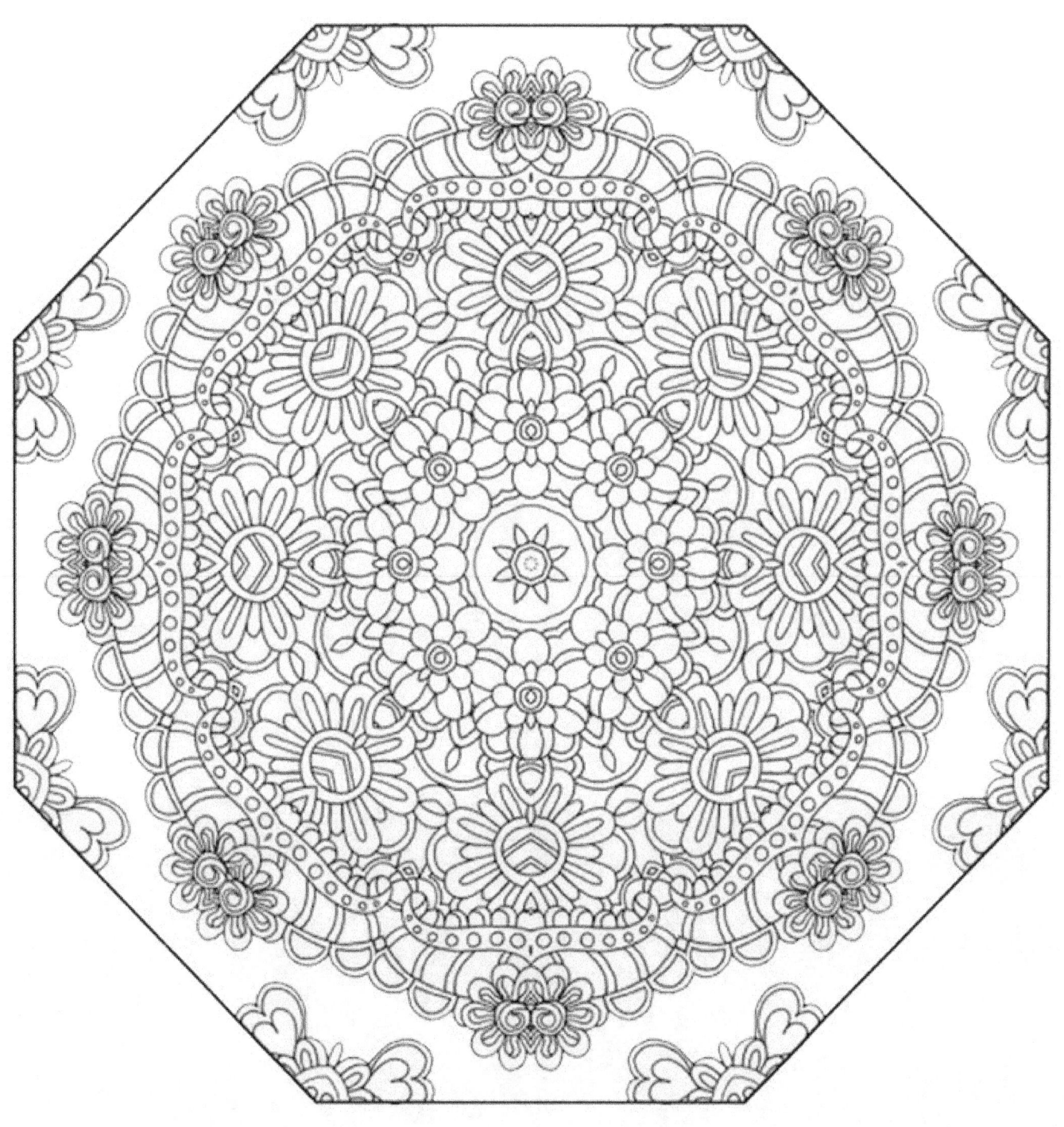

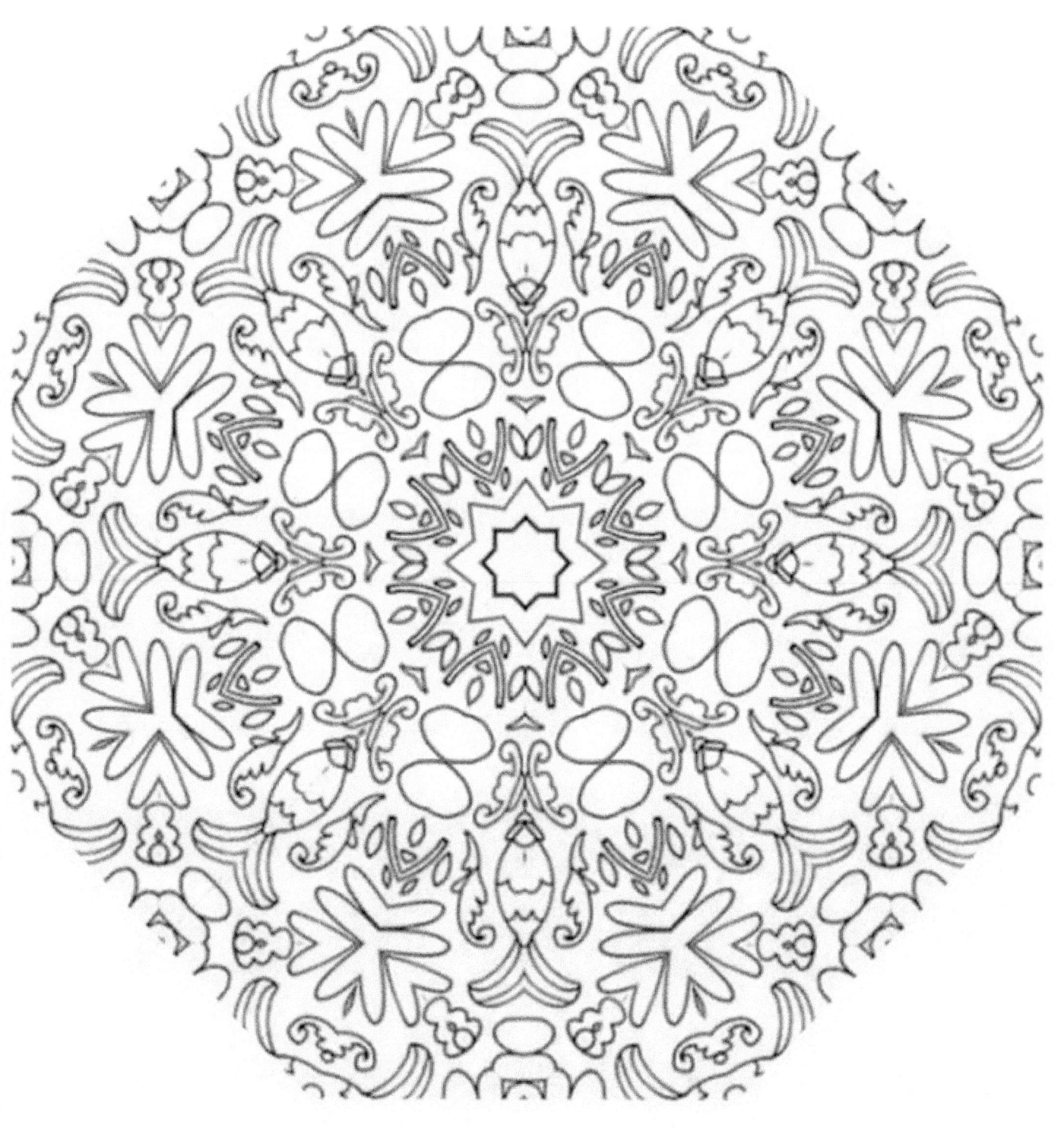

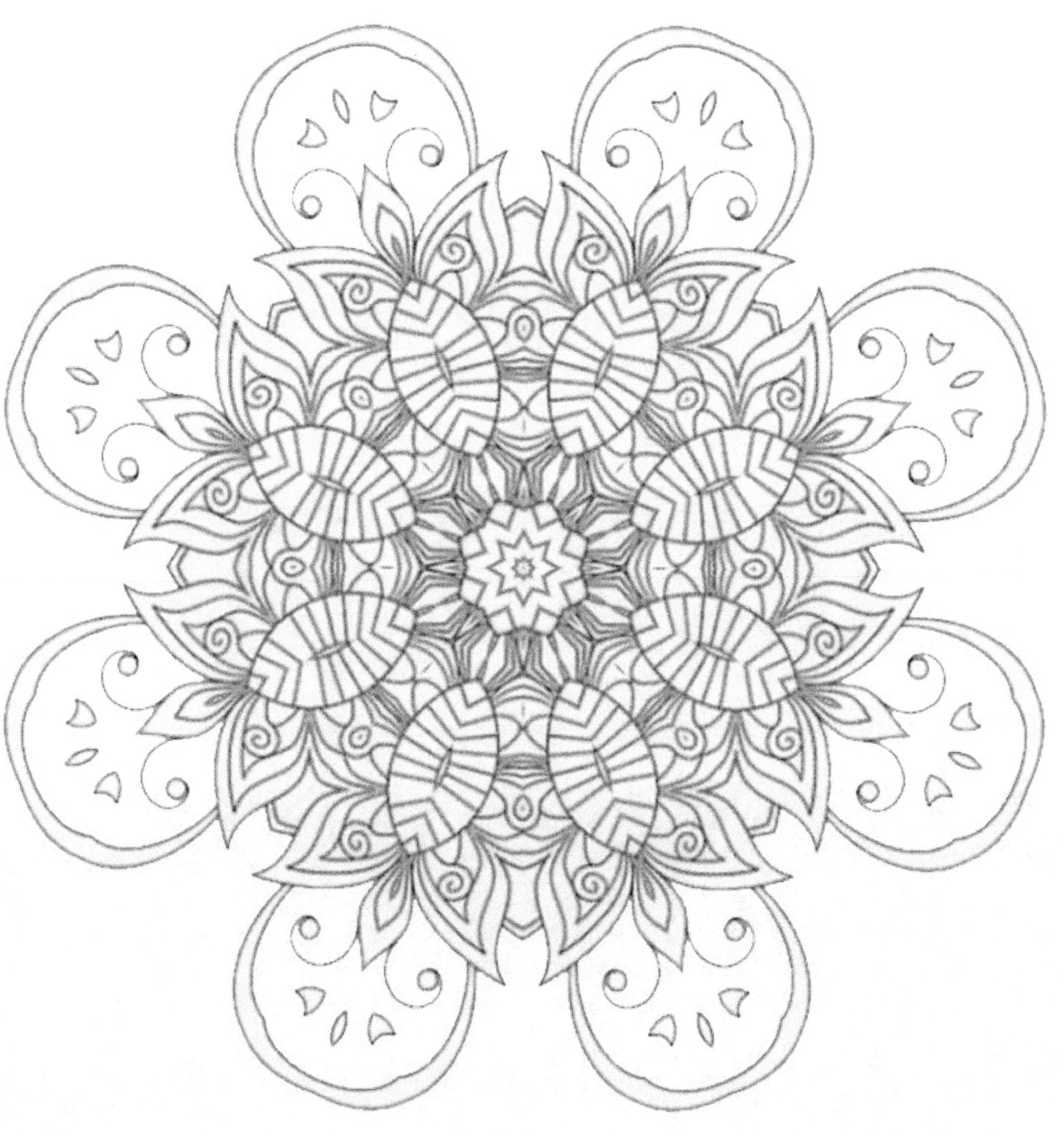

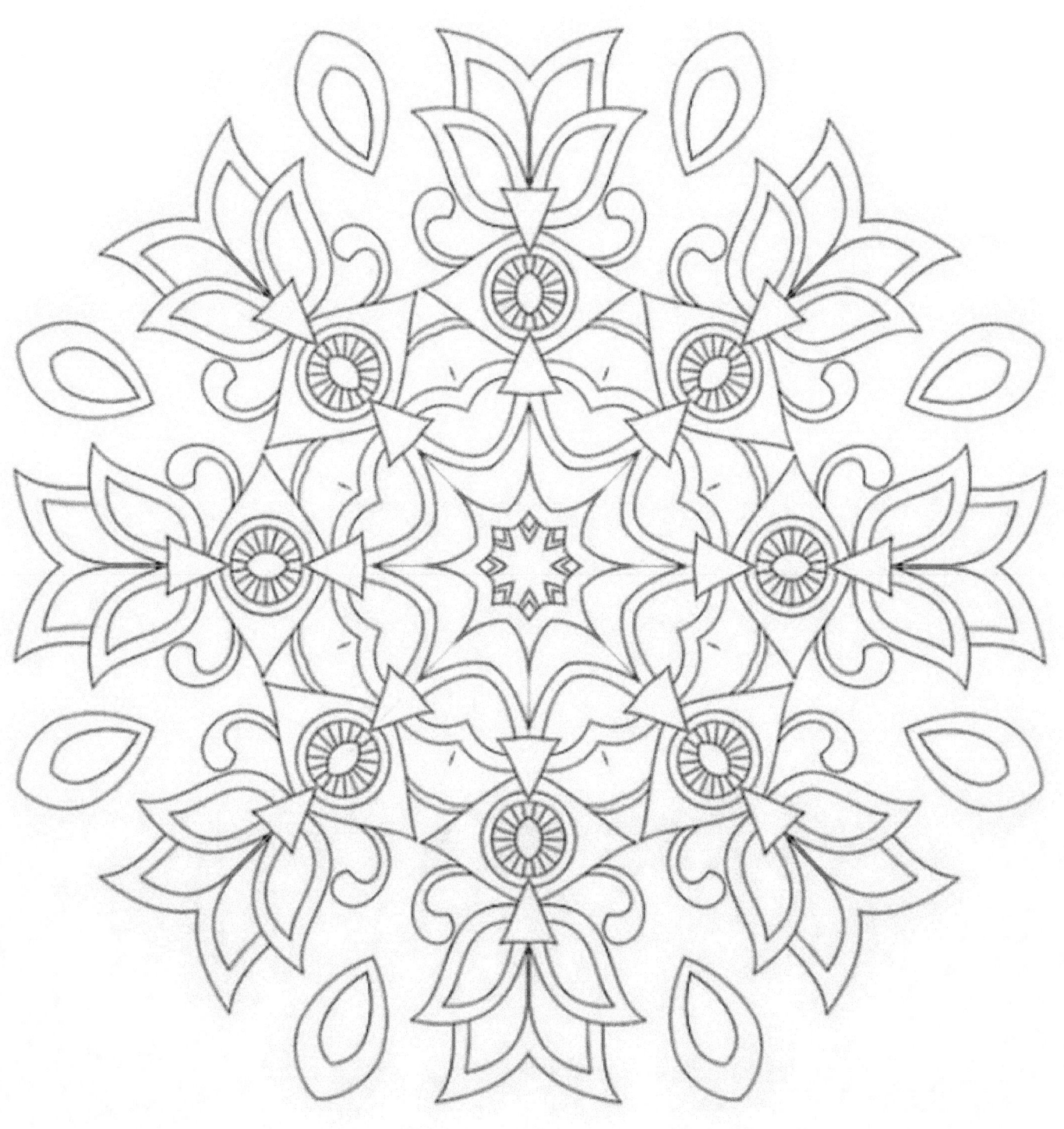

www.ingramcontent.com/pod-product-compliance
Lightning Source LLC
Chambersburg PA
CBHW080619190526
45169CB00009B/3242